UNDERSTANDING GALATIANS

Using Semitic Bible Study Methods with a new foundation

Michael H. Koplitz

Sandra J. Koplitz

This edition 2023 copyright © by Michael H. Koplitz

All Scripture quotations, unless otherwise noted, are taken from the *New American Standard Bible®*, Copyright © 1960, 1962, 1963, 1968, 1971, 1972, 1973, 1975, 1977, 1995 by the Lockman Foundation. Used by permission (www.Lockman.org)

The NASB uses italic to indicate words that have been added for clarification. Citations are shown with large capital letters.

Published by Michael H. Koplitz

Introduction

When a person is baptized as an infant and grows up in the church, different paradigms become a part of their religious DNA. The church has a message to give about Jesus Christ and His importance. Very few people study the theology and doctrines of the church to determine for themselves the accuracy of the church. The Proto-Orthodox church, which survived the pressures of the Roman Empire, decided in its infancy to oppose any expression of Christianity that did not fit its dogma. In addition, the Proto-Orthodox church would permanently destroy any writings that the rival Christians had developed.

The Gnostic Christians of Northern Egypt viewed the life of Jesus of Nazareth in a completely different way than the Proto-Orthodox church did. They saw the message about the Kingdom of Heaven as the vital purpose of Jesus. His birth, death, and Resurrection are not mentioned in the Gnostic Gospels. However, did the Proto-Orthodox church destroy the Gnostic Gospels when they crushed said movement? The answer is yes and no. Yes, they destroyed what they got their hands on. No, because in 1948, copies of the Gnostic religious books were discovered in Alexandria, Egypt. Once these documents were translated, the world learned what the Gnostic Christians believed. It is fascinatingly different than what the Proto-Orthodox said about these followers of Christ.

Why is this understanding critical? Much research points to a different situation in the early years than what the church espouses. A lot of this information is available to anyone today. However, the Seminaries and churches will not openly talk about these other writings about Jesus and His disciples. The scholars teaching in most Seminaries have learned their lessons from the church and from closed-minded mentors who refuse to look at other possibilities. This is because the Western European world took Christianity and changed it from a Near Eastern religion to a Western religion.

There is a theory that Paul converted Mithras House Churches into Jesus House Churches. This is clear from the connection between the Mithras' and Christianity's rituals. For example, baptism was the initiation ritual of Mithras. Communion did not originate with Jesus. This ritual was a part of Mithras where the followers would share his flesh (bread) and drink his blood (wine). There are many more rituals that Christianity picked up from Mithras. A good reference is "Christianity's Need for Mithras," which the author wrote.

Did Paul create the churches in the letters he sent, which comprise the New Testament, and if so, they must have been Jewish groups who became Jewish-Christians? They would have continued with their Hebraic rituals and saw Jesus of Nazareth as the Messiah that the prophets of old had promised. They would have adopted as many as Jesus' teachings and tried to live by them. The letters in the New Testament are written in Greek. However, most Jews in the Roman Empire did not speak Greek; instead, they spoke Aramaic and Hebrew. These congregations would not have understood a Greek letter from Paul.

Therefore, the letters in the New Testament must have been written in Aramaic and then transliterated into Greek. The same can be said for the Gospels, all of them. The church, over the centuries, decided who wrote the Gospels and what their intent was.

The only Gospel we can assign to a writer is Luke. The other three are up in the air about who actually wrote them. While in Seminary, the author was taught that the entire New Testament was originally written in Koine Greek. However, that raised the question of, "Did Jesus speak Greek?" The Seminary instructors said, "no, Jesus did not speak Greek." Then the New Testament, especially the Gospels, must have been written in Aramaic. After all, Jesus spoke Aramaic and Hebrew.

We know this because He was a poor *tekton* (a stonemason or carpenter) from an impoverished city named Nazareth. Being born to a Jewish family in Galilee, he would have learned the traditions of His people and trade. He would have learned to speak Aramaic, the language of the area. He would have learned Hebrew because that was the language of the synagogue and the Temple in Jerusalem. In other words, Hebrew was the language of God, and Jewish males learned the language.

Suppose you are ready to toss this manuscript into the nearest trash can or delete it off your electronic device at this point in the introduction. In that case, the writer has your attention. This is the reaction when the writer has spoken with persons who had been indoctrinated into the church's position since birth. The author did not come into the church environment until he was 35. Therefore, the church's paradigms, dogma, and doctrine were not a part of his DNA. Instead, he questioned a lot. He found many inconsistencies between the Bible and the doctrines of the church. Seminary was an experience to learn what the church had evolved into two-thousand years after the death of Jesus.

There are more parts to the overall premise that the New Testament was originally written in Aramaic and will be explored. For the reader to grasp the subsequent phases of the proof, an open mind is critical.

Culture and Language

Let us continue in the journey of examining the New Testament to determine its original language. Nothing in stone tells us that Aramaic is the Original Language of the New Testament. However, nothing says that Koine Greek was the original language of the New Testament either. Therefore, we have two theories about the original language of the New Testament. The author admits that the Seminary he attended drove home the belief that the Old Testament was written in Hebrew, except for a few spots. The New Testament was initially written in Koine Greek.

The writers' research has been searching for the original meaning of Scripture for many years. The methodology for this work is called "Ancient Bible Study Methods." The method was developed by Dr. Anne Davis of the Bible Learning University in Albuquerque, New Mexico. The author studied this method with Dr. Davis as his mentor. It became clear that the search for the original meaning of the Scriptures requires that the culture and language be examined. So, the author's methodology is Dr. Davis' work, plus his Ph.D. studies combining the method, culture, and language.

The language examination is easy for the Old Testament because it was written in Hebrew, and about one-half of Daniel is in Aramaic. It does not take long to realize that idioms and figures of speech in the Hebrew of the Old Testament revealed a lot about the people and situation of the day when the scrolls were written. The Targums were a valuable resource because they are the Aramaic translations the rabbis did for the people living outside of Judea. The rabbis added commentary to the Targums because they knew that some of the idioms and speech used in the Near East would not translate well into the different areas where the Jews lived.

The culture of the Near East has been essentially the same in many aspects since the days of Jesus. Many practices of Jesus' day are still in use today. The culture of the Jews of the Near East is built into the language. Many times an Aramaic or Hebrew word has a deep meaning that is only fully understood by natives who are living in that culture. The Old Testament is filled with cultural items that do not need to be spelled out because the people knew their culture at the author's time.

Suppose the New Testament in Koine Greek is a transliteration of the Aramaic. The culture, figures of speech, and idioms will be easy to identify when examining the Peshitta (the Aramaic version of the New Testament). Indeed many of the so-called difficult words of Jesus are not tricky when examined in the light of the culture of Jesus' day. An example is, "faith to move a mountain," Jesus said these words to His disciples. The church determined that this meant a complete faith in Jesus. From the western European Greek point of view, that makes sense. What else could it possibly mean?

"Faith to move a mountain" is an Aramaic idiomatic expression. What Jesus said to His followers when he said this is that his disciples needed to be faithful so that they could change the "government's view through their words." The governing body for Judaism resided on the top of a mountain. Jerusalem, with its Temple, was built on the top of Mount Zion, a very tall mountain. This idiom survived because the Aramaic Gospels were transliterated into Koine Greek. Numerous other examples support this position.

Suppose the culture and language idioms of Jesus' day can be found in the Koine Greek because it was transliterated. In that case, it supports the theory of the Aramaic versions being the original language of the Gospels and possibly even more.

The Aramaic Version of the New Testament

The Peshitta is the accepted Aramaic translation of the New Testament for many churches of the East. Peshitta means "simple, true, direct, and original." It is a collection of scrolls that were compiled in 150 CE. There were some revisions to the Peshitta in the fifth and sixth centuries. The Greek version of the New Testament is a transliteration of the Peshitta.[1]

For centuries, the Catholic church has been using the Latin version of the Bible, the Vulgate, and still uses it. The Vulgate was developed around 350 CE by Jerome by order of the Pope at that time. Erasmus (1466 – 1536) was the person who put together the Greek New Testament for the Catholic church.

"The New Testament, brought to light in the original Greek tongue, was compiled and made available for humanity to study and learn. Although working under and deeply associated with the Roman Catholic Church, the learned scholar declared his disagreement with those who wanted to keep the Scriptures from the common people. He said, "If only the farmer would sing something from them at his plow, the weaver moves his shuttle to their tune, the traveler lighten the boredom of his journey with Scriptural stories!" Little did he know, the work he was about to produce would change the world forever. This Greek New Testament, in printed form, would become the standard of the New Testament, launching the translations of Martin Luther and William Tyndale into the world. Thus, fulfilling his dream that all men would read the

---

[1] Rocco A. Errico and George M. Lamsa, *Aramaic Light on Galatians through Hebrews: A Commentary Based on Aramaic, the Language of Jesus, and Ancient near Eastern Customs* (Smyma, GA: Noohra Foundation, 2005).

Bible for themselves in their common language. His new "study Bible" had two main parts, the Greek text, and a revised Latin edition, which was more elegant and accurate than the traditional translation of Jerome's Latin Vulgate. Erasmus prefaced this monumental work of scholarship with an exhortation to Bible study. He proclaimed that the New Testament contains the "philosophy of Christ," simple and accessible teaching with the power to transform lives."[2]

The church recognized Erasmus' Greek New Testament in 1515 CE. The church in the Near East has been using the Peshitta as the original language of the New Testament since 150 CE. If the Greek New Testament was important to the church as an original language, then why did it adopt the Vulgate in 350 CE? The church should have adopted the Greek New Testament at the beginning.

The Peshitta, translated into English, is used to examine Paul's letters. The rest of the methodology that the author developed for Ancient Bible Study Methods is the framework of this research.

---

[2] "Erasmus Greek New Testament," Insight of the King, accessed February 18, 2022, https://www.insightoftheking.com/erasmus-greek-new-testament.html.

The Messianic Tradition Change

One problem for Peter and the Disciples was that they claimed Yeshua to be the Messiah that the prophets of the Hebrew Scriptures spoke of. However, Yeshua did not do what these traditions said. The main tradition was that the Messiah would destroy oppressive Romans and reinstate the Kingdom of Israel. Yeshua would then be declared the king and sit on David's throne in Jerusalem. That did not occur.

None of the messianic traditions of the day worked. So, what was the new movement going to do? They turned to the prophets and discovered Isaiah 50-53. These chapters are referred to as the Suffering Servant chapters. The Yeshua movement decided that the Suffering Servant was Yeshua. The portrayal of Yeshua's life does fit the Suffering Servant chapters. However, rabbinical interpretation then and now sees the Suffering Servant as the nation of Israel. Indeed, these chapters do describe the history of Israel. Nations have wanted to destroy the Jewish people since the time of Abraham.

The diaspora from the Babylonia Exile and the Assyrian invasions looked to squelch the Jewish people. The LORD promised that a remnant of the people would always survive. That is true throughout the 4,000-year history of the Jewish people. Many nations tried to destroy them, and the LORD intervened to ensure that a remnant of the people survived.

Paul must have been convinced in his encounter with Yeshua on the Damascus road that Yeshua was the Suffering Servant. It is clear from Paul's writings that he did believe this. For Paul, the Messiah was the Spiritual Messiah that the Kabbalah spoke. The

Kabbalah says that there will be two Messiahs. This is based on Zachariah 9:9. The first Messiah is Messiah ben Joseph. This Messiah was to restore the Kingdom of Heaven, which is a spiritual Kingdom. The second Messiah will be Messiah ben David. This Messiah was to restore the Kingdom of Israel. The Midrash from the Kabbalah did not state that the Messiah was two different souls.

The Kabbalah

There is a large amount of material in print about the Kabbalah. The Kabbalah referred to is Moses's Secret Work from Mount Sinai. Legends say Moses received three items on Mount Sinai when he met the LORD. The first is the written Law. The written Law is called the Torah. The second is the oral law. The oral law was put into a written form around 200 CE called the Mishnah. The third is the secret law called the Kabbalah. The secrets of the Kabbalah are based on the Torah and were written down around 200 CE. The main books of the Kabbalah are the Zohar and the Book of Creation.

Many of Yeshua's statements have Kabbalah undertones. Yeshua would have known the Kabbalah. Paul would have known the basics, at least, of the Kabbalah because of his religious education and training.

There are Kabbalistic ideas in the Gospels and Paul's letters. Kabbalistic verses will be highlighted in the chapters of the letters.

Methodology

The methodology employed is to use "Ancient Bible Study Methods" integrated with Jesus's day's customs and culture to examine the Hebrew and Christian Scriptures, thus gathering a more in-depth understanding by learning the Scriptures in the way the people of Jesus's day did.

I have titled the methodology of analyzing a passage of Scripture in a Hebraic manner the "Process of Discovery." The author developed this methodology, which brings together various linguistic and cultural understanding areas. There are several sections to the process, and not all the parts apply to every passage of Scripture. The overall result of developing this process is to give the reader a framework for studying the Word in more depth.

The "Process of Discovery" starts with a Scripture passage. An examination of the linguistic structure of the passage is next. The linguistic structure includes parallelism, chiastic structures, and repetition. Formatting the passage in its linguistic form allows the reader to visualize what the first century CE listener was hearing. Their corresponding sections label the chiasms, for example, A, B, C, B', A.' Not all passages of the Scriptures have a poetic form.

The next step is to "question the narrative." The narrative process of questioning the narrative assumes the reader knows nothing about the passage. Therefore, the questions go from the simple to the complex. The next task is to identify any linguistic patterns. Linguistic patterns include, but are not limited to, irony, simile, metaphor, symbolism, idioms, hyperbole, figurative language, personification, and allegory.

A review of any translation inconsistencies discovered between the English NAU version and either the Hebrew or Greek versions is done. There are times when a Hebrew or Greek word is translated in more than one way. Inconsistencies also can be created by the translation committee, which may have decided to use traditional language instead of the actual translation. The decision of the translation committee is in the Preface or Introduction to the Bible. Perhaps some of the inconsistencies were intentionally added to convey some deeper meaning. An examination for every discrepancy is done.

The passage is analyzed for any echoes of the Hebrew Scriptures in the Christian Scriptures. An echo occurs using a passage from the Hebrew Scriptures in the Christian Scriptures.[3] Also, echoes are found when Torah (Genesis through Deuteronomy) passages are used in other Hebrew Bible books. Cross-references in the Scripture are references from one verse to another verse, which can help the reader understand the verse.

The names of persons mentioned in the passage are listed. Many of the Hebrew names have meaning and may be associated with places or actions. Jewish parents used to name their children based on what they felt God had in store for their child. An example of this is Abraham, whose original name was Abram and was changed to mean eternal father (God changed Abram's name to Abraham, indicating a function he was to perform). When the Hebrew Bible gives names, many occurrences mean something unique. The same importance can occur for the names of places. The time it takes to travel between locations can supply insight into the event.

---

[3] Mitzvot are the 613 commandments found in the Torah that please God. There are positive and negative commandments. The list was first development by Maimonides. The full list can be found at: ttp://www.jewfaq.org/613.htm.

Keyphrases are identified in verses when they are essential to understanding that passage. There are no rules for selecting the keywords. Searching for other occurrences of the keywords in Scripture in a concordance is necessary to understand the Word's usage; this must be done in either Hebrew or Greek, not in English. A classic Hebraic approach is to find the usage of a word in the Scripture by finding other verses that contain the Word. The usage of a word in its original language is discovered by searching the Scripture in the language of the Word. Verses that contain the Word are identified, and a pattern for the usage of the Word is discovered. Each verse is examined to see what the usage of the Word is, which may reveal a model for the Word's usage. The first usage of the Word in the Scripture, primarily if used in the Torah, is essential for Hebrew words. For the Greek words, the Christian Scriptures are used to determine the Word usage in the Scripture. Sometimes, it can be very helpful to find the equivalent Greek Word in the Septuagint and then analyze its Hebrew usage.

The Rules of Hillel are used when applicable. Hillel was a Torah scholar who lived shortly before Jesus's day. Hillel developed several rules for Torah students to interpret the Scriptures, which refer to halachic Midrash. In several cases, these rules are helpful in the analysis of the Scripture.

The cultural implications from the writing period are done after the linguistic analysis is completed. The culture is crucial because it is not explicitly referenced in the biblical narratives, as indicated earlier.

From the linguistic analysis and the cultural understanding, it is possible to obtain a deeper meaning of the Scripture beyond the plain text's literal meaning. That is what the listeners of Jesus's time were doing. They put linguistics and culture together without even having to contemplate it.

The analysis will lead to a set of findings explaining what the passage meant in Jesus's day. Most of the time, the Hebraic analysis leads to the desire for more in-depth analysis to fully understand what Jesus was talking about or what was happening to Him. Whatever the result, a new, more in-depth understanding of the Scripture is obtained.

The components of the Process of Discovery are:

Language

Process of Discovery

Linguistics Section

Linguistic Structure

Discussion

Questioning the Passage

Verse Comparison of citations or proof text

Translation Inconsistencies

Biblical Personalities

Biblical Locations

Phrase Study

Linguistic Echoes

Rules of Hillel

Culture Section

Discussion

Questioning the passage

Cultural Echoes

Culture and Linguistics Section

Discussion

Thoughts

Reflections

Only the applicable sections are included in this document.

Introduction

A consensus of scholars believes Paul wrote this letter. The date of the letter is anywhere from 54 to 60 CE. Paul did evangelism in the territory of Galatia. This area was the north-central section of the Galatia, which is modern day Turkey. Tychicus delivered the letter. In the letter, Paul warns the churches that the Gospel of Yeshua needed to be followed as he taught. They were to be wary of the "new" teachings and doctrines that were contrary to what he taught. The Gnostic Christians were the major competing expression of Yeshua's work.

Paul said that faith in Yeshua's death being the way to receive forgiveness of sin and salvation was the true message. The Gnostic said that it was the secret Torah, the lost message, of how to enter heaven that Yeshua brought, is the true way to salvation. Since Paul was converting Mithras House Churches in Galatia by this time, the idea of Yeshua dying for the forgiveness of sins for his followers was the main doctrine of the new Yeshua house churches. Paul did not want his converted churches to learn the ways of the Gnostics, so he made them out to be evil. The Gnostics might have told the people of these churches that they were still pagans because they followed the rituals of Mithras and simply changed the name of their deity.

Paul needed to impress upon the Galatian churches that Yeshua revealed everything to him which made him an apostle equivalent to the original twelve men. Paul deals with several topics in this letter, such as: the church as the body of Christ; Christians are to be justified by faith; salvation of humanity is by God's grace through the Gospel of

Yeshua; sanctification by the Holy Spirit. He also believed that the Jewish legalistic codes, ordinances, and traditions served their purpose and did not have to be followed.[4]

---

[4] Rocco A. Errico and George M. Lamsa, *Aramaic Light on Galatians through Hebrews: A Commentary Based on Aramaic, the Language of Jesus, and Ancient near Eastern Customs* (Smyma, GA: Noohra Foundation, 2005).

Chapter One

Language

Peshitta	New American Standard 1995
Gal. 1:1 Paul, a legate, not from men, nor by man, but by Jesus the Messiah, and God his Father, who raised him from the dead; ² and all the brethren who are with me; unto the churches which are in Galatia. ³ Grace be with you, and peace, from God the Father, and from our Lord Jesus the Messiah; ⁴ who gave himself for our sins, that he might deliver us from this evil world, agreeably to the pleasure of God our Father: ⁵ to whom be glory for ever and ever. Amen. ⁶ I admire, how soon ye have turned from the Messiah, who called you by his grace, unto another gospel; ⁷ which doth not exist, except as there are some who would disquiet you, and are disposed to pervert the gospel of the Messiah. ⁸ But if we, or an angel from heaven, should announce to you differently from what we have announced to you, let him be accursed. ⁹ As I have just said, and now I again say it, that if any one announce to you differently from what ye received, let him be accursed. ¹⁰ For do I now persuade men, or God? Or do I seek to please men? For if I had till now pleased men, I should not have been a servant of the Messiah. ¹¹ But I make known to you, my brethren, that the gospel announced by me, was not from man. ¹² For I did not receive it and learn it from man, but [I had it] by revelation from Jesus the Messiah. ¹³ For ye have heard of my former course of	**Gal. 1:1** Paul, *an apostle (*not *sent* from men nor through the agency of man, but *through Jesus Christ and God the Father, who *raised Him from the dead), ² and all *the brethren who are with me,

To *the churches of Galatia:

Gal. 1:3 *Grace to you and peace from ¹God our Father and the Lord Jesus Christ, ⁴ who *gave Himself for our sins so that He might rescue us from *this present evil ¹age, according to the will of *our God and Father, ⁵ *to whom *be* the glory forevermore. Amen.

Gal. 1:6 I am amazed that you are so quickly deserting *Him who called you ¹by the grace of Christ, for a *different gospel; ⁷ which is *really* not another; only there are some who are *disturbing you and want to distort the gospel of Christ. ⁸ But even if we, or *an angel from heaven, should preach to you a gospel ¹contrary to what we have preached to you, he is to be ²*accursed! ⁹ As we *have said before, so I say again now, *if any man is preaching to you a gospel ¹contrary to what you received, he is to be ²*accursed!

Gal. 1:10 For am I now *seeking the favor of men, or of God? Or am I striving to please men? If I were still trying to please |

life in Judaism, that I persecuted the church of God exceedingly, and destroyed it: [14] and that I went much farther in Judaism than many of my contemporaries who were of my nation, and was peculiarly zealous for the doctrine of my fathers. [15] But when it pleased him, who separated me from my mother's womb, and called me by his grace, [16] to reveal his Son by me, that I should proclaim him among the Gentiles; forthwith, I did not open it to flesh and blood; [17] nor did I go to Jerusalem, to them who were legates before me; but I went into Arabia, and returned again to Damascus: [18] and after three years, I went to Jerusalem to see Cephas; and I remained with him fifteen days. [19] But others of the legates I saw not, except James, our Lord's brother. [20] In the things which I am writing to you, behold, before God! I lie not. [21] And after that, I went to the regions of Syria and Cilicia. [22] And the churches in Judaea which were in the Messiah; did not know me personally: [23] but this only had they heard, that he who before persecuted us, now preacheth that faith which in time preceding he subverted: [24] and they glorified God in me.

men, I would not be a [b]bond-servant of Christ.

Gal. 1:11 For [a]I would have you know, brethren, that the gospel which was preached by me is [b]not according to man. [12] For [a]I neither received it from man, nor was I taught it, but *I received it* through a [b]revelation of Jesus Christ.

Gal. 1:13 For you have heard of [a]my former manner of life in Judaism, how I [b]used to persecute [c]the church of God beyond measure and [d]tried to destroy it; [14] and I [a]was advancing in Judaism beyond many of my contemporaries among my [1]countrymen, being more extremely zealous for my [b]ancestral traditions. [15] But when God, who had set me apart *even* from my mother's womb and [a]called me through His grace, was pleased [16] to reveal His Son in me so that I might [a]preach Him among the Gentiles, [b]I did not immediately consult with [1][c]flesh and blood, [17] [a]nor did I go up to Jerusalem to those who were apostles before me; but I went away to Arabia, and returned once more to [b]Damascus.

Gal. 1:18 Then [a]three years later I went up [b]to Jerusalem to [1]become acquainted with [c]Cephas, and stayed with him fifteen days. [19] But I did not see any other of the apostles except [1][a]James, the Lord's brother. [20] (Now in what I am writing to you, [1]I assure you [a]before God that I am not lying.) [21] Then [a]I went into the regions of [b]Syria and [c]Cilicia. [22] I was *still* unknown by [1]sight to [a]the churches of Judea which were [b]in Christ; [23] but only, they kept

	hearing, "He who once persecuted us is now preaching [a]the faith which he once [b]tried to destroy." **24** And they [a]were glorifying God [1]because of me.

References to the New American Standard 1995

Galatians 1:1
[a]2 Cor 1:1
[b]Gal 1:11f
[c]Acts 9:15; Gal 1:15f
[d]Acts 2:24

Galatians 1:2
[a]Phil 4:21
[b]Acts 16:6; 1 Cor 16:1

Galatians 1:3
[1]Two early mss read *God the Father, and our Lord Jesus Christ*
[a]Rom 1:7

Galatians 1:4
[1]Or *world*
[a]Gal 2:20
[b]Matt 13:22; Rom 12:2; 2 Cor 4:4
[c]Phil 4:20

Galatians 1:5
[a]Rom 11:36

Galatians 1:6
[1]Lit *in*
[a]Rom 8:28; Gal 1:15; 5:8
[b]2 Cor 11:4; Gal 1:7, 11; 2:2, 7; 5:14; 1 Tim 1:3

Galatians 1:7
[a]Acts 15:24; Gal 5:10

Galatians 1:8
[1]Or *other than, more than*
[2]Gr *anathema*
[a]2 Cor 11:14
[b]Rom 9:3

Galatians 1:9

[1]Or *other than, more than*
[2]Gr *anathema*
[a]Acts 18:23
[b]Rom 16:17
[c]Rom 9:3

Galatians 1:10
[a]1 Cor 10:33; 1 Thess 2:4
[b]Rom 1:1; Phil 1:1

Galatians 1:11
[a]Rom 2:16; 1 Cor 15:1
[b]1 Cor 3:4; 9:8

Galatians 1:12
[a]1 Cor 11:23; Gal 1:1
[b]1 Cor 2:10; 2 Cor 12:1; Gal 1:16; 2:2

Galatians 1:13
[a]Acts 26:4f
[b]Acts 8:3; 22:4, 5
[c]1 Cor 10:32
[d]Acts 9:21

Galatians 1:14
[1]Lit *race*
[a]Acts 22:3
[b]Jer 9:14; Matt 15:2; Mark 7:3; Col 2:8

Galatians 1:15
[a]Is 49:1, 5; Jer 1:5; Acts 9:15; Rom 1:1; Gal 1:6

Galatians 1:16
[1]I.e. human beings
[a]Acts 9:15; Gal 2:9
[b]Acts 9:20
[c]Matt 16:17

Galatians 1:17
[a]Acts 9:19-22
[b]Acts 9:2

Galatians 1:18
[1]Or *visit Cephas*
[a]Acts 9:22f
[b]Acts 9:26
[c]John 1:42; Gal 2:9, 11, 14

Galatians 1:19
[1]Or *Jacob*
[a]Matt 12:46; Acts 12:17

Galatians 1:20
[1]Lit *behold before God*
[a]Rom 9:1; 2 Cor 1:23; 11:31

Galatians 1:21
[a]Acts 9:30
[b]Acts 15:23, 41
[c]Acts 6:9

Galatians 1:22
[1]Lit *face*
[a]1 Cor 7:17; 1 Thess 2:14
[b]Rom 16:7

Galatians 1:23
[a]Acts 6:7; Gal 6:10
[b]Acts 9:21

Galatians 1:24
[1]Lit *in me*
[a]Matt 9:8

Koine Greek

Gal. 1:1 Παυλος αποστολος ουκ απ' ανθρωπων, ουδε δι' ανθρωπου, αλλα δια Ιησου χριστου, και θεου πατρος του εγειραντος αυτον εκ νεκρων, [2] και οι συν εμοι παντες αδελφοι, ταις εκκλησιαις της Γαλατιας· [3] χαρις υμιν και ειρηνη απο θεου πατρος, και κυριου ημων Ιησου χριστου, [4] του δοντος εαυτον περι των αμαρτιων ημων, οπως εξεληται ημας εκ του ενεστωτος αιωνος πονηρου, κατα το θελημα του θεου και πατρος ημων· [5] ω η δοξα εις τους αιωνας των αιωνων αμην.

Gal. 1:6 Θαυμαζω οτι ουτως ταχεως μετατιθεσθε απο του καλεσαντος υμας εν χαριτι χριστου εις ετερον ευαγγελιον· [7] ο ουκ εστιν αλλο, ει μη τινες εισιν οι ταρασσοντες υμας και θελοντες μεταστρεψαι το ευαγγελιον του χριστου. [8] Αλλα και εαν ημεις η αγγελος εξ ουρανου ⸀ ευαγγελιζηται ⸀ υμιν παρ' ο ευηγγελισαμεθα υμιν, αναθεμα εστω. [9] Ως προειρηκαμεν, και αρτι παλιν λεγω, ει τις υμας ευαγγελιζεται παρ' ο παρελαβετε, αναθεμα εστω. [10] Αρτι γαρ ανθρωπους πειθω η τον θεον; Η ζητω ανθρωποις αρεσκειν; Ει γαρ ετι ανθρωποις ηρεσκον, χριστου δουλος ουκ αν ημην.

Gal. 1:11 Γνωριζω δε υμιν, αδελφοι, το ευαγγελιον το ευαγγελισθεν υπ' εμου, οτι ουκ εστιν κατα ανθρωπον. [12] Ουδε γαρ εγω παρα ανθρωπου παρελαβον αυτο, ουτε εδιδαχθην, αλλα δι' αποκαλυψεως Ιησου χριστου. [13] Ηκουσατε γαρ την εμην αναστροφην ποτε εν τω Ιουδαισμω, οτι καθ' υπερβολην εδιωκον την εκκλησιαν του θεου, και επορθουν αυτην· [14] και προεκοπτον εν τω Ιουδαισμω υπερ πολλους συνηλικιωτας εν τω γενει μου, περισσοτερως ζηλωτης υπαρχων των πατρικων μου παραδοσεων. [15] Οτε δε ευδοκησεν ο θεος ο αφορισας με εκ κοιλιας μητρος μου και καλεσας δια της χαριτος αυτου, [16] αποκαλυψαι τον υιον αυτου εν εμοι, ινα ευαγγελιζωμαι αυτον εν τοις εθνεσιν, ευθεως ου προσανεθεμην σαρκι και αιματι· [17] ουδε ανηλθον εις Ιεροσολυμα προς τους προ εμου αποστολους, αλλα απηλθον εις Αραβιαν, και παλιν υπεστρεψα εις Δαμασκον.

Gal. 1:18 Επειτα μετα ετη τρια ανηλθον εις Ιεροσολυμα ιστορησαι Πετρον, και επεμεινα προς αυτον ημερας δεκαπεντε. [19] Ετερον δε των αποστολων ουκ ειδον, ει μη Ιακωβον τον αδελφον του κυριου. [20] Α δε γραφω υμιν, ιδου ενωπιον του θεου οτι ου ψευδομαι. [21] Επειτα ηλθον εις τα κλιματα της Συριας και της Κιλικιας. [22] Ημην δε αγνοουμενος τω προσωπω ταις εκκλησιαις της Ιουδαιας ταις εν χριστω· [23] μονον δε ακουοντες ησαν οτι Ο διωκων ημας ποτε, νυν ευαγγελιζεται την πιστιν ην ποτε επορθει. [24] Και εδοξαζον εν εμοι τον θεον.

Language
  Process of Discovery

   Linguistics Section

    Linguistic Structure

[Introduction] Gal. 1:1   Paul, [a]an apostle ([b]not *sent* from men nor through the agency of man, but [c]through Jesus Christ and God the Father, who [d]raised Him from the dead), **2** and all [a]the brethren who are with me, to [b]the churches of Galatia: **Gal. 1:3**   [a]Grace to you and peace from [1]God our Father and the Lord Jesus Christ, **4** who [a]gave Himself for our sins so that He might rescue us from [b]this present evil [1]age, according to the will of [c]our God and Father, **5** [a]to whom *be* the glory forevermore. Amen.

[Condemnation] Gal. 1:6   I am amazed that you are so quickly deserting [a]Him who called you [1]by the grace of Christ, for a [b]different gospel; **7** which is *really* not another; only there are some who are [a]disturbing you and want to distort the gospel of Christ. **8** But even if we, or [a]an angel from heaven, should preach to you a gospel [1]contrary to what we have preached to you, he is to be [2b]accursed! **9** As we [a]have said before, so I say again now, [b]if any man is preaching to you a gospel [1]contrary to what you received, he is to be [2c]accursed!

[Paul's authority[Gal. 1:10   For am I now [a]seeking the favor of men, or of God? Or am I striving to please men? If I were still trying to please men, I would not be a [b]bond-servant of Christ. **Gal. 1:11**   For [a]I would have you know, brethren, that the gospel which was preached by me is [b]not according to man. **12** For [a]I neither received it from man, nor was I taught it, but *I received it* through a [b]revelation of Jesus Christ. **Gal. 1:13**   For you have heard of [a]my former manner of life in Judaism, how I [b]used to persecute [c]the church of God beyond measure and [d]tried to destroy it; **14** and I [a]was advancing in Judaism beyond many of my contemporaries among my [1]countrymen, being more extremely zealous for my [b]ancestral traditions.

[Yeshua's calling] **15** But when God, who had set me apart *even* from my mother's womb and [a]called me through His grace, was pleased **16** to reveal His Son in me so that I might [a]preach Him among the Gentiles, [b]I did not immediately consult with [1c]flesh and blood, **17** [a]nor did I go up to Jerusalem to those who were apostles before me; but I went away to Arabia, and returned once more to [b]Damascus. **Gal. 1:18**   Then [a]three years later I went up [b]to Jerusalem to [1]become acquainted with [c]Cephas, and stayed with him fifteen days. **19** But I did not see any other of the apostles except [1a]James, the Lord's brother. **20** (Now in what I am writing to you, [1]I assure you [a]before God that I am not lying.) **21** Then [a]I went into the regions of [b]Syria and [c]Cilicia. **22** I was *still* unknown by [1]sight to [a]the churches of Judea which were [b]in Christ; **23** but only, they kept hearing,

"He who once persecuted us is now preaching [a]the faith which he once [b]tried to destroy." **24** And they [a]were glorifying God [l]because of me.

Discussion

Paul gives the reason that he believed that he had authority to oversee this congregation.

Questioning the Passage

1. Where was Paul when he wrote this letter? (v. 1)

    It is difficult to determine where Paul was located when he wrote the letter because an exact date of the letter is not possible.

2. Had Paul visited the church before writing the letter? (v. 1)

    Acts 16:6-10 says that Paul traveled in the territory.

"A.D. 51 or 52: — The form of the Greek expression implies that Phrygia and Galatia are not to be regarded as separate districts — but the land originally inhabited by Phrygians, but subsequently occupied by Cauls. Paul does not appear to have had any intention of preaching the gospel here. He was perhaps anxious at once to bear his message to the more important and promising district of proconsular Asia. But he was detained by a return of his old malady "the thorn in the flesh" — some sharp and violent attack which humiliated him and prostrated his physical strength. To this the Galatians owed their knowledge of Christ. Though a homeless, stricken wanderer might seem but a feeble advocate of a cause so momentous, yet it was the Divine order that in the preaching of the gospel strength should be made perfect in weakness. The zeal of the preacher and the enthusiasm of his hearers triumphed over all impediments. They did not despise the temptation in his flesh. They received him as an angel of God, even as Christ Jesus. They would have plucked out their very eyes if they could and have given them to him." It can scarcely have been any predisposing religious sympathy which attracted them so powerfully. The gospel as a message of mercy and a spiritual faith stood in direct contrast to the gross and material religions in which the race had been nurtured. But if we picture to ourselves the apostle, as he appeared before the Galatians, a friendless outcast, writhing under the tortures of a painful malady, yet instant in season and out of season, by turns denouncing and entreating, perhaps also, as at Lystra, enforcing his appeals by some striking miracle, we shall be at no loss to conceive how the fervid temperament of the Gaul might have been aroused. In the absence of all direct testimony we may conjecture that it was at Ancyra, now the capital of the Roman province, as formerly of the Gaulish settlement, "the most illustrious metropolis," as it is called in formal documents; at Pessinus under the shadow of Mount Dindimus, the cradle of the worship of Cybele, and one of the principal commercial towns of the district; at Tavium, at once a strong fortress and a great emporium, situated at the point of convergence of several important roads; perhaps also at Juliopolis, the ancient Gordium, formerly the capital of Phrygia, almost equidistant from the three seas, and from its central position a busy mart; at these, or some of these places, that Paul founded the earliest Churches of Galatia"[5]

---

[5] Paul's first visit to Galatia, A.D. 51 or 52, accessed March 27, 2023, https://biblehub.com/sermons/auth/lightfoot/paul's_first_visit_to_galatia_ad_51_or_52.htm.

3. Who brought the Gospel to Galatia? (v. 1)

    According to Acts 16:6-10 Paul did.

4. What is the implication that Paul said that Yeshua died for sin? (v. 4)

    By Yeshua's death and resurrection, he made known that sin and malevolent forces have no power of those who walk in the way of the LORD. Yeshua used the power of meekness, lovingkindness, and nonresistance. Yeshua freed those who live according to His teaching from the evils that humans have created. Therefore, the phrase "Yeshua died for the forgiveness of sin" originally meant that he died to bring us the ways to please the LORD. That way is to follow the LORD's ways, which are found in the Torah. Yeshua exemplified the Torah by fulfilling it. This meant that everything Yeshua said and did was in alignment with the Torah. Therefore, Yeshua died because he brought the message of peace and love to an evil world. To follow Yeshua's ways is to follow the Torah, as exemplified by Yeshua. However, for converted Mithras House churches, it was believed that Mithras died for the forgiveness of his follower's sin. By Paul substituting Yeshua for Mithras, the atonement theology became that Yeshua died for the forgiveness of sin for his followers.

5. How is a person set free from the evil age because of Yeshua's death? (v. 4)

    Paul does not offer any explanation for his atonement position. If Paul wrote to a Mithras converted church, this would explain his atonement position. It was a main theological feature of the Mithras cult that Mithras died for the forgiveness of sins. Since Paul does not explain this idea, it can be concluded that the Mithras cult doctrine was left in place. The Jewish concept of the Messiah did not include the Messiah dying for the forgiveness of sin for the people. Rather, the Jewish Messianic tradition was that the Messiah would restore the spiritual awareness and understanding to the people of the LORD.

6. Who are the outside influences that were trying to change the Galatians' churches? (v. 6-9)

There were at least two groups of people that Paul was concerned about. One was Jewish-Christians from Judea. These followers believed that the Torah and the Jewish laws had to be followed to be a disciple of Yeshua's teaching. The concern here is that if the church was a converted Mithras church (as almost all were) then the Jewish ways infiltrating the church would be radically different from the ways of Mithras. This would cause a conflict in the churches. The other group would have been the Gnostic Christians. They believed Yeshua brought the message of how to get into Heaven, which was lost over the centuries. Yeshua's birth and death were irrelevant. It was Yeshua's words and actions that mattered. For a Mithras converted church, this would have been a problem since they were told that Yeshua replaced Mithras and that Yeshua himself brought forgiveness for sin by dying on the Cross.

7. Why is Arabia mentioned? (v. 17)

The Arabian desert was a place for retreat and to gain inspiration. Many of the LORD's prophets went to the Arabian desert to commune with the LORD before starting their work. The book of Acts does not mention that Paul went to Arabia after meeting the LORD on the Damascus Road. The idea of visiting Arabia was probably added because, after Yeshua's baptism, he went there. This statement links Paul and Yeshua.

8. Why did Paul say he returned to Damascus when he never mentioned it? (v. 17)

   Damascus had become the headquarters for the Yeshua movement in the Near East. Therefore, Paul said that he was going back to headquarters. He did not have to mention that he was there in order to return. It can be inferred that he went to Damascus to meet with other leaders of the movement.

9. Why did the translation committee use the word Cephas instead of Rock which was Peter's nickname? (v. 18)

   The Greek and Aramaic versions of the verse use the name Cephas. By calling him Cephas, Paul was rebuking Peter as the leader of the group. There was a tension between Paul and Peter from the beginning of Paul's conversion. Paul wanted no requirements for the Gentiles to enter the movement. That was necessary for the Mithras Cult conversions. Peter wanted to keep the movement more Hebraic and wanted followers to become proselytes before becoming followers.

10. What is the significance of fifteen days (v. 18)

    "The meaning of the number 15 in the Bible is rest. This rest comes after deliverance that is represented by fourteen. The 15th day of the first Hebrew month (Nisan) is the first day of the Feast of Unleavened Bread, a day of rest for the children of Israel (and for Christians). The 15th day of the seventh Hebrew month begins the Feast of Tabernacles, also a day of rest.

    God, as the sun set to begin Nisan 15, informed in a vision that his descendants would end up as slaves in a foreign country (Egypt). They would, however, eventually be set free (Genesis 15:12 - 16).

Many years later in Egypt, God miraculously delivered Israel's firstborn from the death angel just as Passover began after sunset (Nisan 14). Then, 24 hours later (just as the sun was setting to begin Nisan 15), the children of Israel began to leave Egypt (Exodus 12:40 - 41). This night is referred to as the 'night to be much observed' (Exodus 12:40 - 42, Deuteronomy 16:1). God's prophecy of freedom, given to Abraham on Nisan 15, was fulfilled years later on the exact same day."[6]

11. Why does Paul take an oath in verse twenty?

Paul assured the Galatians church that his letter was his words and were not influenced by Peter or anyone else. The Jerusalem church had a strong influence on the early Proto-Orthodox church. Paul is showing his belief that he was an apostle and could carry Christ's message without having to confirm anything with anybody.

12. What is the value of verse twenty-two?

Paul's conversion on the Damascus Road was apparently not reported to the Jerusalem church immediately. Paul was seen as the persecutor of the church at that time. It is also possible that the Jerusalem church did not believe in his conversion. Paul could have been leading them into a trap.

---

[6] "Home," Bible Study, accessed March 27, 2023, https://www.biblestudy.org/bibleref/meaning-of-numbers-in-bible/15.html.

13. What does verse twenty-four say about Paul's personality?

Paul had an ego-centered personality. He liked to take credit at every opportunity.

Culture Section

Discussion

The term "chosen me from my birth" does not mean predestination. It is a Near Eastern expression which means that the LORD knows what is in the hearts of people before they are formed and what they are going to do from birth to death. The LORD can see a person's entire lifespan. In the Near East, boys were dedicated to the LORD's work before they were born. Mothers made pledges that their prospective male child would serve the LORD.[7]

Thoughts

This is an introduction to the letter. It cannot be determined if Paul visited this church in particular. He was in the territory that this church was in. But did he establish this congregation is hard to tell. The introduction he offers is comprehensive but explains a few items that the people would have known if Paul was there earlier. Clearly, the church is a Mithras converted church because the main theme of Yeshua dying for sins matches what the Mithras cult believed Mithras did. Paul does his usual grabbing of credit for the Yeshua movement. With Mithras church conversions, he deserves the credit for that work since he did it.

---

[7] Rocco A. Errico and George M. Lamsa, *Aramaic Light on Galatians through Hebrews: A Commentary Based on Aramaic, the Language of Jesus, and Ancient near Eastern Customs* (Smyrna, GA: Noohra Foundation, 2005).

Chapter Two

Language

Peshitta	New American Standard 1995
Gal. 2:1 And again, after fourteen years, I went up to Jerusalem with Barnabas; and I took with me Titus. **2** And I went up by revelation: and I explained to them the gospel which I announce among the Gentiles; and I stated it to them who were esteemed prominent, between myself and them: lest I should have run, or might run in vain. **3** Also Titus, who was with me, and was a Gentile, was not compelled to be circumcised. **4** And in regard to the false brethren, who had crept in to spy out the liberty we have in Jesus the Messiah, in order to bring me under subjection; **5** not for the space of an hour, did we throw ourselves into subjection to them; so that the truth of the gospel might remain with you. **6** And they who were esteemed prominent, (what they were, I care not; for God regardeth not the persons of men,)— even these persons added nothing to me. **7** But, otherwise; for they saw, that the gospel of the uncircumcision was intrusted to me, as to Cephas was intrusted that of the circumcision. **8** For he that was operative with Cephas in the legateship of the circumcision, was also operative with me in the legateship of the Gentiles. **9** And James, Cephas, and John, who were accounted pillars, when they perceived the grace that was given to me, gave to me and Barnabas the right hand of fellowship; that we [should labor] among the Gentiles, and	**Gal. 2:1** Then after an interval of fourteen years I [a]went up again to Jerusalem with [b]Barnabas, taking [c]Titus along also. **2** [1]It was because of a [a]revelation that I went up; and I submitted to them the [b]gospel which I preach among the Gentiles, but *I did so* in private to those who were of reputation, for fear that I might be [c]running, or had run, in vain. **3** But not even [a]Titus, who was with me, though he was a Greek, was [b]compelled to be circumcised. **4** But *it was* because of the [a]false brethren secretly brought in, who [b]had sneaked in to spy out our [c]liberty which we have in Christ Jesus, in order to [d]bring us into bondage. **5** But we did not yield in subjection to them for even an hour, so that [a]the truth of the gospel would remain with you. **6** But from those who [1]were of high [a]reputation (what they were makes no difference to me; [b]God [2]shows no partiality) — well, those who were of reputation contributed nothing to me. **7** But on the contrary, seeing that I had been [a]entrusted with the [b]gospel [1]to the uncircumcised, just as [c]Peter *had been* [2]to the circumcised **8** (for He who effectually worked for Peter in *his*

they among the circumcision. **10** Only [they desired] that we would be mindful of the needy; and I was solicitous to do the same. **11** But when Cephas was come to Antioch, I rebuked him to his face; because they were stumbled by him. **12** For before certain ones came from James, he ate with the Gentiles: but when they came, he withdrew himself, and separated; because he was afraid of them of the circumcision. **13** And the rest of the Jews also were with him in this thing; insomuch that even Barnabas was induced to regard persons. **14** And when I saw, that they did not walk correctly, in the truth of the gospel, I said to Cephas, before them all: If thou art a Jew, and livest in the Gentile way, and not in the Jewish, why dost thou compel the Gentiles to live in the Jewish way? **15** For if we, who are Jews by nature, and are not sinners of the Gentiles, **16** because we know that a man is not made just by the works of the law, but by faith in Jesus the Messiah; even we have believed in Jesus the Messiah, in order to be made just by faith in the Messiah, and not by the works of the law: for, by the deeds of the law, no flesh is made just. **17** And if, while we seek to become just by the Messiah, we are found to be ourselves sinners, is Jesus the Messiah therefore the minister of sin? Far be it! **18** For if I should build up again the things I had demolished, I should show myself to be a transgressor of the precept. **19** For I, by the law, have become dead to the law, that I might live to God; and I am crucified with the Messiah. **20** And henceforth it is no more I who live, but the Messiah liveth in me: and the life I now live in the flesh, I live by faith in the Son of God, who loved me and gave himself

[a]apostleship [1]to the circumcised effectually worked for me also to the Gentiles), **9** and recognizing [a]the grace that had been given to me, [1b]James and [c]Cephas and John, who were [d]reputed to be [e]pillars, gave to me and [f]Barnabas the [g]right [2]hand of fellowship, so that we *might* [h]*go* to the Gentiles and they to the circumcised. **10** *They* only *asked* us to remember the poor — [a]the very thing I also was eager to do.

Gal. 2:11 But when [a]Cephas came to [b]Antioch, I opposed him to his face, because he [1]stood condemned. **12** For prior to the coming of certain men from [1a]James, he used to [b]eat with the Gentiles; but when they came, he *began* to withdraw and hold himself aloof, [c]fearing [2]the party of the circumcision. **13** The rest of the Jews joined him in hypocrisy, with the result that even [a]Barnabas was carried away by their hypocrisy. **14** But when I saw that they [a]were not [1]straightforward about [b]the truth of the gospel, I said to [c]Cephas in the presence of all, "If you, being a Jew, [d]live like the Gentiles and not like the Jews, how *is it that* you compel the Gentiles to live like Jews? [2]

Gal. 2:15 "We *are* [a]Jews by nature and not [b]sinners from among the Gentiles; **16** nevertheless knowing that [a]a man is not justified by the works of [1]the Law but through faith in Christ Jesus, even we have believed in Christ Jesus, so that we may be justified by [b]faith in Christ and not by the works of [1]the Law; since [c]by the works of [1]the Law no [2]flesh will be justified. **17** "But

for me. [21] I do not spurn the grace of God. For if righteousness is by means of the law, the Messiah died in vain.	if, while seeking to be justified in Christ, we ourselves have also been found [a]sinners, is Christ then a minister of sin? [b]May it never be! [18] "For if I rebuild what I have *once* destroyed, I [a]prove myself to be a transgressor. [19] "For through [1]the Law I [a]died to [1]the Law, so that I might live to God. [20] "I have been [a]crucified with Christ; and it is no longer I who live, but [b]Christ lives in me; and [1]the *life* which I now live in the flesh I live by faith in [c]the Son of God, who [d]loved me and [e]gave Himself up for me. [21] "I do not nullify the grace of God, for [a]if righteousness *comes* through [1]the Law, then Christ died needlessly."

References to the New American Standard 1995

Galatians 2:1
[a]Acts 15:2
[b]Acts 4:36; Gal 2:9, 13
[c]2 Cor 2:13; Gal 2:3

Galatians 2:2
[1]Lit *according to revelation I went up*
[a]Acts 15:2; Gal 1:12
[b]Gal 1:6
[c]Rom 9:16; 1 Cor 9:24ff; Gal 5:7; Phil 2:16; 2 Tim 4:7; Heb 12:1

Galatians 2:3
[a]2 Cor 2:13; Gal 2:1
[b]Acts 16:3; 1 Cor 9:21

Galatians 2:4
[a]Acts 15:1, 24; 2 Cor 11:13, 26; Gal 1:7
[b]2 Pet 2:1; Jude 4
[c]Gal 5:1, 13; James 1:25
[d]Rom 8:15; 2 Cor 11:20

Galatians 2:5
[a]Gal 1:6; 2:14; Col 1:5

Galatians 2:6
[1]Lit *seemed to be something*
[2]Lit *does not receive a face*
[a]2 Cor 11:5; 12:11; Gal 2:9; 6:3
[b]Acts 10:34

Galatians 2:7
[1]Lit *of the uncircumcision*
[2]Lit *of the circumcision*
[a]1 Cor 9:17; 1 Thess 2:4; 1 Tim 1:11
[b]Acts 9:15; Gal 1:16
[c]Gal 1:18; 2:9, 11, 14

Galatians 2:8
[1]Lit *of the circumcision*

*a*Acts 1:25

Galatians 2:9
[1]Or *Jacob*
[2]Lit *hands*
*a*Rom 12:3
*b*Acts 12:17; Gal 2:12
*c*Luke 22:8; Gal 1:18; 2:7, 11, 14
*d*2 Cor 11:5; 12:11; Gal 2:2, 6; 6:3
*e*1 Tim 3:15; Rev 3:12
*f*Acts 4:36; Gal 2:1, 13
*g*2 Kin 10:15
*h*Gal 1:16

Galatians 2:10
*a*Acts 24:17

Galatians 2:11
[1]Or *was to be condemned;* lit *was one who was condemned,* or, *was self-condemned*
*a*Gal 1:18; 2:7, 9, 14
*b*Acts 11:19; 15:1

Galatians 2:12
[1]Or *Jacob*
[2]Or converts *from the circumcised;* lit *those from the circumcision*
*a*Acts 12:17; Gal 2:9
*b*Acts 11:3
*c*Acts 11:2

Galatians 2:13
*a*Acts 4:36; Gal 2:1, 9

Galatians 2:14
[1]Or *progressing toward;* lit *walking straightly*
[2]Some close the direct quotation here, others extend it through v 21
*a*Heb 12:13
*b*Gal 1:6; 2:5; Col 1:5
*c*Gal 1:18; 2:7, 9, 11
*d*Acts 10:28; Gal 2:12

Galatians 2:15
*a*Phil 3:4f

[b]1 Sam 15:18; Luke 24:7

Galatians 2:16
[1]Or *law*
[2]Or *mortal man*
[a]Acts 13:39; Gal 3:11
[b]Rom 3:22; 9:30
[c]Ps 143:2; Rom 3:20

Galatians 2:17
[a]Gal 2:15
[b]Luke 20:16; Gal 3:21

Galatians 2:18
[a]Rom 3:5

Galatians 2:19
[1]Or *law*
[a]Rom 6:2; 7:4; 1 Cor 9:20

Galatians 2:20
[1]Or *insofar as I*
[a]Rom 6:6; Gal 5:24; 6:14
[b]Rom 8:10
[c]Matt 4:3
[d]Rom 8:37
[e]Gal 1:4

Galatians 2:21
[1]Or *law*
[a]Gal 3:21

Koine Greek

Gal. 2:1   Επειτα δια δεκατεσσαρων ετων παλιν ανεβην εις Ιεροσολυμα μετα Βαρναβα, συμπαραλαβων και Τιτον· ² ανεβην δε κατα αποκαλυψιν, και ανεθεμην αυτοις το ευαγγελιον ο κηρυσσω εν τοις εθνεσιν, κατ᾽ ιδιαν δε τοις δοκουσιν, μηπως εις κενον τρεχω η εδραμον. ³ Αλλ᾽ ουδε Τιτος ο συν εμοι, Ελλην ων, ηναγκασθη περιτμηθηναι· ⁴ δια δε τους παρεισακτους ψευδαδελφους, οιτινες παρεισηλθον κατασκοπησαι την ελευθεριαν ημων ην εχομεν εν χριστω Ιησου, ινα ημας καταδουλωσωνται· ⁵ οις ουδε προς ωραν ειξαμεν τη υποταγη, ινα η αληθεια του ευαγγελιου διαμεινη προς υμας. ⁶ Απο δε των δοκουντων ειναι τι οποιοι ποτε ησαν ουδεν μοι διαφερει· προσωπον θεος ανθρωπου ου λαμβανει εμοι γαρ οι δοκουντες ουδεν προσανεθεντο· ⁷ αλλα τουναντιον, ιδοντες οτι πεπιστευμαι το ευαγγελιον της ακροβυστιας, καθως Πετρος της περιτομης _ ⁸ ο γαρ ενεργησας Πετρω εις αποστολην της περιτομης, ενηργησεν και εμοι εις τα εθνη _ ⁹ και γνοντες την χαριν την δοθεισαν μοι, Ιακωβος και Κηφας και Ιωαννης, οι δοκουντες στυλοι ειναι, δεξιας εδωκαν εμοι και Βαρναβα κοινωνιας, ινα ημεις ῾ μεν ᾿ εις τα εθνη, αυτοι δε εις την περιτομην· ¹⁰ μονον των πτωχων ινα μνημονευωμεν, ο και εσπουδασα αυτο τουτο ποιησαι.

Gal. 2:11 Οτε δε ηλθεν Πετρος εις Αντιοχειαν, κατα προσωπον αυτω αντεστην, οτι κατεγνωσμενος ην. ¹² Προ του γαρ ελθειν τινας απο Ιακωβου, μετα των εθνων συνησθιεν· οτε δε ηλθον, υπεστελλεν και αφωριζεν εαυτον, φοβουμενος τους εκ περιτομης. ¹³ Και συνυπεκριθησαν αυτω και οι λοιποι Ιουδαιοι, ωστε και Βαρναβας συναπηχθη αυτων τη υποκρισει. ¹⁴ Αλλ᾽ οτε ειδον οτι ουκ ορθοποδουσιν προς την αληθειαν του ευαγγελιου, ειπον, τω Πετρω εμπροσθεν παντων, Ει συ, Ιουδαιος υπαρχων, εθνικως ζης και ουκ Ιουδαικως, τι τα εθνη αναγκαζεις Ιουδαιζειν; ¹⁵ Ημεις φυσει Ιουδαιοι και ουκ εξ εθνων αμαρτωλοι, ¹⁶ ειδοτες οτι ου δικαιουται ανθρωπος εξ εργων νομου, εαν μη δια πιστεως Ιησου χριστου, και ημεις εις χριστον Ιησουν επιστευσαμεν, ινα δικαιωθωμεν εκ πιστεως χριστου, και ουκ εξ εργων νομου· διοτι ου δικαιωθησεται εξ εργων νομου πασα σαρξ. ¹⁷ Ει δε, ζητουντες δικαιωθηναι εν χριστω, ευρεθημεν και αυτοι αμαρτωλοι, αρα χριστος αμαρτιας διακονος; Μη γενοιτο. ¹⁸ Ει γαρ α κατελυσα, ταυτα παλιν οικοδομω, παραβατην εμαυτον συνιστημι. ¹⁹ Εγω γαρ δια νομου νομω απεθανον, ινα θεω ζησω. ²⁰ Χριστω συνεσταυρωμαι· ζω δε, ουκετι εγω, ζη δε εν εμοι χριστος· ο δε νυν ζω εν σαρκι, εν πιστει ζω τη του υιου του θεου, του αγαπησαντος με και παραδοντος εαυτον υπερ εμου. ²¹ Ουκ αθετω την χαριν του θεου· ει γαρ δια νομου δικαιοσυνη, αρα χριστος δωρεαν απεθανεν.

Language

Process of Discovery

Linguistics Section

Linguistic Structure

[Paul goes to Jerusalem] Gal. 2:1 Then after an interval of fourteen years I [a]went up again to Jerusalem with [b]Barnabas, taking [c]Titus along also. **2** [1]It was because of a [a]revelation that I went up; and I submitted to them the [b]gospel which I preach among the Gentiles, but *I did so* in private to those who were of reputation, for fear that I might be [c]running, or had run, in vain. **3** But not even [a]Titus, who was with me, though he was a Greek, was [b]compelled to be circumcised. **4** But *it was* because of the [a]false brethren secretly brought in, who [b]had sneaked in to spy out our [c]liberty which we have in Christ Jesus, in order to [d]bring us into bondage. **5** But we did not yield in subjection to them for even an hour, so that [a]the truth of the gospel would remain with you. **6** But from those who [1]were of high [a]reputation (what they were makes no difference to me; [b]God [2]shows no partiality) — well, those who were of reputation contributed nothing to me. **7** But on the contrary, seeing that I had been [a]entrusted with the [b]gospel [1]to the uncircumcised, just as [c]Peter *had been* [2]to the circumcised **8** (for He who effectually worked for Peter in *his* [a]apostleship [1]to the circumcised effectually worked for me also to the Gentiles), **9** and recognizing [a]the grace that had been given to me, [1b]James and [c]Cephas and John, who were [d]reputed to be [e]pillars, gave to me and [f]Barnabas the [g]right [2]hand of fellowship, so that we *might* [b]go to the Gentiles and they to the circumcised. **10** *They* only *asked* us to remember the poor — [a]the very thing I also was eager to do.

[Peter to Antioch] Gal. 2:11 But when [a]Cephas came to [b]Antioch, I opposed him to his face, because he [1]stood condemned. **12** For prior to the coming of certain men from [1a]James, he used to [b]eat with the Gentiles; but when they came, he *began* to withdraw and hold himself aloof, [c]fearing [2]the party of the circumcision. **13** The rest of the Jews joined him in hypocrisy, with the result that even [a]Barnabas was carried away by their hypocrisy. **14** But when I saw that they [a]were not [1]straightforward about [b]the truth of the gospel, I said to [c]Cephas in the presence of all, "If you, being a Jew, [d]live like the Gentiles and not like the Jews, how *is it that* you compel the Gentiles to live like Jews? [2]

[The Law] Gal. 2:15 "We *are* [a]Jews by nature and not [b]sinners from among the Gentiles; **16** nevertheless knowing that [a]a man is not justified by the works of [1]the Law but through faith in Christ Jesus, even we have believed in Christ Jesus, so that we may be justified by [b]faith in Christ and not by the works of [1]the Law; since [c]by the works of [1]the Law no [2]flesh will be justified. **17** "But if, while seeking to be justified in Christ, we ourselves have also been found *a*sinners, is Christ then a minister of sin? *b*May it never be! **18** "For if I rebuild what I have *once* destroyed, I *a*prove myself to be a transgressor. **19** "For through [1]the Law I *a*died to [1]the Law, so that I might live to God. **20** "I have been *a*crucified with Christ; and it is no longer I who live, but *b*Christ lives in me; and [1]the *life* which I now live in the flesh I live by faith in *c*the Son of God, who *d*loved me and *e*gave Himself up for me. **21** "I do not nullify the grace of God, for *a*if righteousness *comes* through [1]the Law, then Christ died needlessly."

Discussion

Questioning the Passage

1. What is the significance of the number of fourteen? (v. 1)

   The number fourteen in the New Testament signifies salvation. "On day 14 of the first month (Nisan) in 30 A.D. Jesus Christ, God manifested in the flesh, the only begotten Son of God the Father, and the Lamb of God to take away the sin of the world, was crucified as the perfect sacrifice to save humanity from sin."[8]

2. What is the revelation? (v. 2)

   Paul wanted it to be clear that he did not go to Jerusalem because of any human motivation. Paul believed revelations were from the LORD and gave specific directions.[9]

3. Who were these men of reputation? (v. 2)

   This is the way Paul addressed the leadership of the Jerusalem church.

---

[8] "Home," Bible Study, accessed April 2, 2023, https://www.biblestudy.org/bibleref/meaning-of-numbers-in-bible/14.html.

[9]

4. Is there a difference in Paul's Gospel? (v. 2)

    Since Paul was insistent that none of the Jewish laws needed to be followed by Gentiles that his message of the Gospel was different. In the respect to the Mithras church conversions that Paul accomplished, he would not have been able to convert them by forcing Jewish Law on the Mithras house churches. No one in those churches would have known Jewish Law nor would they want to change their ways. The change in the deity in the Mithras church was common throughout history. However, the rituals and basic beliefs did not change.

5. What does "running or had run, in vain" mean? (v. 2)

    "In vain" is used by Paul in his letters as an advert meaning "without effect." The term "run" (in Greek) stems from the athletic imagery of that day. Paul uses it as a metaphor for strenuous exertion in living the Christian life.[10]

6. Why is it important that Paul said Titus was not compelled to be circumcised? (v. 3)

    Paul wanted to show that the Peter requirement of circumcision was unnecessary. He presented Titus as a follower of Yeshua without circumcision.

7. Who are the spies, and what were they doing? (v. 4)

    The spies are persons who believed in a unique expression of Christianity. It is known that the Gnostic Christians from North Africa were infiltrating Paul's converted churches to get them to follow the Gnostic expression and not the Mithras converted expression of who Yeshua was and what he represented.

---

[10] IBID.

8. Explain verse five?

"5 οἷς οὐδὲ πρὸς ὥραν εἴξαμεν τῇ ὑποταγῇ, "we did not give in to them in this matter even for a moment." The Western text, together with such church fathers as Tertullian (*Adv. Marc.* 5.3.3) and Irenaeus (*Adv. Haer.* 3.13.3), omits οἷς οὐδέ, thereby reading "we gave in for a moment." The omission may have been accidental at first, but soon became used to support the view that Titus was circumcised (see above on v 3). Marcion, of course, retained οὐδέ, but omitted οἷς, which conforms to his insistence that Paul never made any concession to anyone, either to false brothers or to the Jerusalem apostles— who in his view were much the same. Both omissions, however, seem tendentious, and so unable to overturn the negative reading οἷς οὐδέ that is attested by all the Greek uncial MSS (except D*), p⁴⁶, all the versions (except it^{d,e}), and all the Greek church fathers (except Irenaeus in Latin translation).

The expression πρὸς ὥραν is an idiom meaning "for a short time"—or more colloquially "for a moment." It appears elsewhere in Paul at 2 Cor 7:8, 1 Thess 2:17; Philem 15 (cf. John 5:35; *Mart. Pol.* 11:2; see also Matt 10:19 [Luke 12:12]; 26:40 [Mark 14:37]; 26:45 [Mark 14:41]; 26:55 for illustrations of the flexible use of ὥρα). The aorist εἴξαμεν with the negative states the simple fact of history, "we did not yield" or "give in" to them. The dative noun ὑποταγῇ ("by way of subjection") is somewhat redundant, amplifying as it does εἴξαμεν, and so perhaps unnecessary to translate. The article before ὑποταγῇ, however, suggests a particular subjection that was being demanded and that Paul refused, which calls for some such translation as "in this matter" in order to specify."[11]

---

[11] Longenecker, R. N. (1990). *Galatians* (Vol. 41, p. 52). Word, Incorporated.

It should be noted that different bishops and theologians of the Church changed the actual text to meet their needs. Therefore, the truth of the Gospel changed over the centuries. Would Yeshua even recognize what his original disciples started after his ascension? Probably not. 90% of the rituals of today's Christianity was a part of the Mithras cult. Since it has been established by scholars that the Greek New Testament was changed to fit the theological desires of church bishops, it is difficult to know what Paul's original intent was. The Peshitta needs to become the church's standard. Very little change occurred to the Peshitta over the centuries and the earliest copy is from 150 CE.

9. Why does the name change from Peter to Cephas in the Greek version but not in the Peshitta in verse nine?

   Scholars do not have a good reason for the name change in verse nine. There is the possibility that a redactor changed this verse. The Peshitta does not have the different name. If Paul used Cephas instead of Peter, it could be to downplay Peter. If the Galatian church knew Simon (his given name) as Peter and Paul did not want to show his influence, he then used Cephas. Cephas is the Aramaic nickname Yeshua gave Peter. The name Peter comes from the English phonic of the Greek word Πετρος. The nickname Cephas has a Greek equivalent Κηφας which means "rock." Cephas in the Aramaic language means rock. It is unknown why Paul used the two different names.

10. Why is Titus missing from the grace given? (v. 9)

   It is odd that Titus is missing. Titus was a Gentile. The names listed in the verse are all Jews. For Paul to say that Titus did not receive grace because he was not a Jew would have discounted his argument that Gentile followers of Yeshua had to be circumcised. Therefore, it is not clear why Paul neglected to mention Titus. It could be a simple error of forgetfulness.

11. Why are the poor mentioned in verse ten?

"The expression τῶν πτωχῶν ("the poor"), which here is a genitive of reference and the true predicate of the sentence, has also been moved forward for emphasis. Its articular form signals its absolute use: either (1) those financially impoverished (cf. Josephus, *J. W.* 569–70, where οἱ ἄποροι, "the lower classes," equals οἱ πτωχοί, "the poor"), or (2) those adhering to a special kind of Jewish piety (so-called anawim piety from the Hebrew adjective עָנִי, *ʿānî*), where "poor" suggests not only economic impoverishment but also carries honorific nuances of "humility," "obedience," and "piety" before God."[12]

The Jewish piety, in Paul's case, at this point in his life, is his faith in saving grace of Yeshua. He could be referring to people who are poor in spirit because they have been given the opportunity to follow Yeshua or those who rejected that idea.

12. Why did Cephas go to Antioch? (v. 11)

During Paul's time, his headquarter was in Antioch.

"When Cephas came to Antioch" implies a well-known visit of Cephas to the city—not a return of its first bishop, but a visit known to both Paul and his Galatian addressees. Jews frequently traveled between Jerusalem and Antioch

---

[12] Longenecker, R. N. (1990). *Galatians* (Vol. 41, p. 59). Word, Incorporated.

(see C. H. Kraeling, *JBL* 51 [1932] 130–60), and Jewish Christians did likewise (see Acts 11:19–26, 30; 15:1–4, 22, 30; 18:22). Was, then, Cephas's visit something of an occasional visit? Was it a stopover on his way to somewhere else? Or was it where he went to escape persecution at Jerusalem (cf. Acts 12:17, "then he left [Jerusalem] for another place")? We just do not know, though by the way Paul alludes to the visit, we may believe that both Paul and his addressees did."[13]

13. What is the difference between verse 11 in Peshitta and NASB?

Paul rebuked Peter because he strongly disagreed with the idea that the Gentiles needed to be circumcised to become followers of Yeshua. The NASB directly says that Paul said Peter was wrong.

14. Why is Cephas afraid of the Christian Jews because he ate un-kosher food? (v. 12)

Peter wanted more for Gentiles to be circumcised to join the fellowship. He wanted them to follow the Torah Laws. The story about him being in Lebanon and eating non-kosher food makes him out to be a hypocrite. He was probably concerned about being confronted with this issue.

15. Why was the term "the circumcised" used in verse twelves and "Jews" used in thirteen?

The term "the circumcised" referred to Peter and his followers. "Jews" were the rest of the tribe.

---

[13] Longenecker, R. N. (1990). *Galatians* (Vol. 41, pp. 71–72). Word, Incorporated.

16. Why did Paul toss out the Torah? (v. 16)

Paul had to dismiss the Torah when he was converting Gentiles to Christianity as he envisioned it. The accessibility of copies of the Torah was a problem. The Hebrew Scriptures were not available in large quantities. Paul gave the Gentiles enough verses from the prophets that predict the coming of the Jewish Messiah. If Paul pressed the Torah laws, he would not have been successful. Paul went to Jewish synagogues and was unsuccessful. When he turned to the Mithras House churches, he was successful in convincing them that Yeshua was the real son of God and not Mithras. He did not change the Mithras rituals. He left those rituals in place. This would explain why over 90% of today's Christian rituals are identical to the Mithras rituals. The Torah laws also would have eliminated several foods that the Gentiles depended on, especially pork. Pork was inexpensive in Paul's day and was a major supply of protein for the Gentile population.

17. What does it mean to be justified in Christ? (v. 17)

It is the belief that just having faith that Yeshua was resurrected by the LORD three days after his death allows all of your sins to be forgiven. The process is called atonement. There are many atonement doctrines in Christianity.

18. What does verse eighteen mean?

"The argument here is a type of contrary reasoning: "If I do what I shouldn't, then I am." The sentence is cast in the form of a first class conditional sentence, not a second class contrary-to-fact condition, probably because Paul has in mind Peter and certain other Jewish Christians who in one way or another seemed intent on doing just that, even though terribly inconsistent in so doing. The use of the first person singular suffix ("I") in the three verbs of the sentence (cf. also the reflexive pronoun ἐμαυτόν, "myself"), as opposed to the first person plural ("we") of v 17 (cf. also the plural intensive pronoun αὐτοί), is a rhetorical feature that allows Paul to make his point in more diplomatic fashion—i.e., by applying to himself a charge really directed against others."[14]

19. What does verse twenty mean?

This verse draws on mysticism. "Mysticism, of course, frequently conjures up ideas about the negation of personality, withdrawal from objective reality, ascetic contemplation, a searching out of pathways to perfection, and absorption into the divine—all of which is true for Eastern and Grecian forms of mysticism. The mysticism of the Bible, however, affirms the true personhood of people and all that God has created in the natural world, never calling for negation or withdrawal except where God's creation has been contaminated by sin. Furthermore, the mysticism of biblical religion is not some esoteric searching for a path to be followed that will result in union with the divine, but is always of the nature of a response to God's grace wherein people who have been mercifully touched by God enter into communion with him without ever losing their own identities. It is, as H. A. A. Kennedy once called it, "that contact between the human and the Divine which forms the core of the deepest religious experience, but which can only be felt as an immediate intuition of the highest reality and cannot be described in the language of psychology" (*The Theology of the Epistles*, 122)."[15]

---

[14] Longenecker, R. N. (1990). *Galatians* (Vol. 41, p. 90). Word, Incorporated.

[15] IBID.

20. Why is Yeshua called Christ and the Son of God in verse twenty?

The mysticism of Christianity is that Yeshua is the Messiah and is the son of God. The phrase "son of God" can be assigned to those who follow the LORD's wishes. It was a well used phrased in Yeshua's and Paul's day.

21. How is verse twenty-one justified against Yeshua's word about fulfilling the Law?

Many Jews accused Paul of neglecting the Torah, which was believed to offer the grace of the LORD. He is attempting to say that he still believed in the Torah.

Biblical Personalities

1. Barnabas – "In the book of Acts, we find a Levite from Cyprus named Joses (Acts 4:36), whom the apostles called Barnabas. That nickname, translated "Son of Encouragement" (Acts 4:36-37) or "Son of Exhortation" was probably given to him because of his inclination to serve others (Acts 4:36-37, 9:27) and his willingness to do whatever church leaders needed (Acts 11:25-30). He is referred to as a "good man, full of the Holy Spirit and faith." Through his ministry, "a great number of people were brought to the Lord" (Acts 11:24). Paul uses Barnabas as an example of one with a proper perspective on money and property. When he sold his land, he brought the proceeds to the apostles and laid it at their feet (Acts 4:36-37).

As the early church began to grow, in spite of Herod's persecution, Barnabas was called by the Holy Spirit to go with Paul on a missionary journey. Barnabas' cousin, John Mark, served him and Paul as their assistant (Acts 13:5). During that first missions trip, for an unspecified reason, John Mark left them and did not complete the journey (Acts 13:13). However, Barnabas continued with Paul and was with him when Paul's ministry was redirected to reaching the Gentiles with the gospel (Acts 13:42-52). The only negative mention of Barnabas in Scripture is in reference to an incident in which Peter's hypocrisy influenced other Jews (including Barnabas) to shun some Gentiles at dinner (Galatians 2:13)."[16]

2.   Titus – "Titus was one of at least two younger men that Paul discipled and described as his "son in the faith that we share" (Titus 1:4). The other man is Timothy, and the second letter to the Corinthians is addressed as from Paul and Timothy to the church in Corinth (2 Corinthians 1:1). Both Timothy and Titus served as Paul's messengers and traveling companions, and they both went on to lead churches. Paul not only mentored them, but he also advised them in individual letters about their next steps.

Titus' background is not explained, other than the fact he was Gentile and apparently never circumcised (Galatians 2:4). This is an interesting point, since Timothy was half-Greek, and not circumcised either. Still, Paul chose to circumcise Timothy to honor the Jews in an area that the two of them were ministering in (Acts 16:1-5). Paul repeatedly mentions in his letters that circumcision is not necessary under the new covenant, and even tells Titus to silence Christians who try to promote it (Titus 1:10-14). So, Paul's choice to circumcise Timothy would suggest that he had a pragmatic side. He did not require his disciples to be circumcised, but if the situation called for working among Jews and it made things easier, he would concede to it. Whether Titus

---

[16] GotQuestions.org, "Home," GotQuestions.org, February 5, 2010, https://www.gotquestions.org/life-Barnabas.html.

ever ministered to Jewish believers is not stated, and both he and Titus worked at churches in Gentile areas (Timothy in Ephesus, Titus in Crete, and Corinth and Dalmatia)."[17]

Biblical Locations

1. Antioch – "After defeating his rival Antigonus at the battle of Ipsus in 301 B.C., and thereby winning full control of Syria for himself, Seleucus founded four "sister cities" in northwestern Syria: Antioch and its port city Seleucia Pieria; Apamea and its port city Laodicea of the Sea. These cities were founded in order to play a primary role in the subjugation of the conquered territory and were settled by Macedonians and Greeks in order to assure the transplantation of Greek culture onto Semitic soil. Seleucia Pieria, named for Seleucus himself, was built first and was originally meant to be the capital city of the Seleucids because of its highly defensible position. Before long, however, principally because of its better location on the inland trade routes, Antioch eclipsed Seleucia Pieria in importance, as it did also the other cities of the Seleukis (i.e., the quadruplet of cities founded by Seleucus in northwestern Syria). Soon after Seleucus' death in 280 B.C., Antiochus I Soter (280–261 B.C.), his son, established Antioch as the Seleucid royal city and capital.

Seleucid Antioch was built by the architect Xenarius, with elephants from Seleucus' army stationed to mark the location of towers in the city wall and wheat used to lay out the streets. The city was laid out in an oblong plan of about 555 acres (slightly less than a square mile) between the river to the west and the main trade route to the east, being set far enough away from Mt. Silpius

---

[17] "Who Was Titus in the Bible - Book of Titus in the Bible," biblestudytools.com, December 21, 2022, https://www.biblestudytools.com/bible-study/topical-studies/who-was-titus-in-the-bible-and-why-should-you-read-his-book-now.html.

(farther to the east) so as not to be inundated by sediment and gravel brought down from the mountain by the winter rains. Like many other Greek cities, Seleucid Antioch was constructed on the Hippodamus plan, with streets crossing each other at right angles and buildings placed in the rectangles formed by the streets. The city was laid out to make the best use of the sun in both winter and summer, and so that the winds that blew up the Orontes valley from the sea could penetrate all its sections. The *agora*, or market, was situated along the east side of the river and probably was about eight city blocks in size. A citadel for protection was located to the east at the top of Mt. Silpius.

Five miles to the south on an elevated plateau with flowing springs and lush vegetation was the small town of Daphne. Though it was located on a site too small for a city, Daphne's amenities attracted many residents and visitors, and it soon became a flourishing suburb of Antioch. Royalty spent their summers at Daphne, enjoying its scenery, cool air, and clear, clean water. The wealthy built villas, private baths, and pleasure houses there. The famous Temple of Apollo was erected in the most beautiful part of Daphne, near the constantly flowing springs that were diverted into two streams around the shrine. Ordinary people took their pleasures in the precincts of the Temple of Apollo, in the public baths, and in the restaurants and colonnades where refreshment and entertainment were provided. There was also a large and fine theater located on the western slope of the Daphne plateau, which was built to take advantage of the contours of the land.

The original population of Antioch was made up of retired Macedonian soldiers of Seleucus' army, of Athenians who had been transferred from Antigonia (Antigonus's capital) and resettled at Antioch, of Jews who had served as mercenaries in the Seleucid army, and of slaves of diverse origins. In addition, there were native Syrians who were assigned a separate section in the city. Altogether, from various records and the excavations conducted from 1932–39, it seems fair to say that the free population of Antioch during its early Seleucid days numbered somewhere between 17,000 and 25,000—plus slaves and native Syrians, who were not counted.

Antiochus I enlarged Antioch to include a sizable second quarter east of the main trade route and up to the base of Mt. Silpius, a new section which he protected from the wash down the mountain by diverting the waters around the city. After his death, the Ptolemies of Egypt controlled northern Syria and the city of Antioch for about two decades. Taking the city back again, Seleucus II Callinicus (246–226 B.C.) enlarged Antioch by building a third quarter northwest of the existing city on a large island in the middle of the Orontes River (the island was completely wiped away by the earthquakes of the sixth century A.D.). The greed of Antiochus III "the Great" (223–187 B.C.), however, brought him into conflict with Rome, with the result that he was defeated at the battle of Magnesia (190 B.C.) and lost all of his empire beyond the Taurus range to the Romans or to kingdoms allied with the Romans (like Pergamum). This was a turning point in the history of the Seleucid empire, though not the end of the fame and fortunes of Antioch.

Antiochus IV Epiphanes (176–163 B.C.) was the last of the great Seleucid rulers. Under his reign the broad slope of Mt. Silpius became the fourth and main quarter of the city, meriting the title "Tetrapolis" or "Fourth City." In this new section of the city Antiochus IV built a new senate house and several new temples. After Antiochus IV, however, bloody internal struggles for the throne exhausted the economy of the Seleucids, and Antioch never regained its former splendor until the Romans came."[18]

---

[18] Longenecker, R. N. (1990). *Galatians* (Vol. 41, pp. 65–67). Word, Incorporated.

Phrase Study

1. **δοκεω** (v.6)
   a) to consider as probable, *think, believe, suppose, consider,* trans., of subjective
   b) to appear to one's understanding, *seem, be recognized as*

Culture Section

Discussion

Paul probably went to Jerusalem for the Feast of the Pentecost (Shavuos). This was one of the three festivals that people traveled to Jerusalem. On such occasions, friends and enemies met to settle feuds and quarrels. Paul was warned not to go to Jerusalem because there were many people angry with him. It was during such a festival that he was arrested and sent to Rome for trial.

Titus was an Aramean whose mother was Jewish. Jewish women who married Gentile men continued to practice their religion, traditions, and customs. Therefore, Titus was considered a Greek but was raised to respect Jewish customs, laws and the LORD.

Circumcision was an identification mark to distinguish the descendants of Abraham from the other peoples of the world. Yeshua's original disciples were loyal to Jewish customs and taught that circumcision was necessary. Paul viewed this practice as an ancient Hebraic tradition that was unnecessary for new Gentiles to be a part of the Yeshua movement.

"They of the circumcision" refers to Jewish followers of Yeshua. This term was used to distinguish between converts from the Jewish religion and those from the Mithras (or other pagan) religion.

Peter, James, and John became the leaders of the Yeshua movement after Yeshua's death. They sent a spiritual letter about the problems of faith of the Antioch Christians. There were unnecessary disputes between the faithful. They also instructed the people to not eat the blood of animals.

In the Near East, brothers and relatives of holy men were greatly revered. James, the son of Zebedee, was one of the closest disciples of Yeshua. He became a major leader of the church in Jerusalem until he was murdered. Paul took orders from Jesus' brother, James. This letter says that James' power and authority was feared more than the other apostles. This is a reason Paul did not listen to Peter.

The customs and manners of countries played a role when a prophet was preaching in that country. There were time were the customs and manners obscured their message. It also explains why a prophet from one country was not understood in a different country.

According to ancient bible laws, justification and salvation were obtained through the works of the law that regulated all aspects of life. It is the following of the Laws in the Torah that offer salvation. However, it is not possible to follow every law perfectly. That is why the LORD placed repentance (teshuva) into the Torah. The LORD knew the people cannot follow every Law successfully.

"I am crucified with Christ" means that "I share the sufferings that Christ endured on the cross because I live according to his way of life."

Thoughts

It is sad that Paul and Peter destroyed the unity that Yeshua desired for humanity after his life. Paul was totally against everything that the Jerusalem church decided. Christianity might have died out if Paul did not disobey. However, the idea of disobedience and defiance became a part of the DNA of the church. That would explain the over 1000 denominations in Christianity today and the mainline denominations that are splitting apart today.

Chapter Three

Language

Peshitta	New American Standard 1995
Gal. 3:1 O ye Galatians, deficient in understanding! Who hath fascinated you? For lo, Jesus the Messiah hath been portrayed as in a picture, crucified before your eyes. **2** This only would I learn from you, Was it by works of the law, that ye received the Spirit? or by the hearing of faith? **3** Are ye so foolish, that having begun in the Spirit, ye now would consummate in the flesh? **4** And have ye borne all these things in vain? And I would, it were in vain! **5** He therefore who giveth the Spirit in you, and who worketh miracles among you, [doth he these things] by the deeds of the law? or by the hearing of faith? **6** In like manner Abraham believed God, and it was accounted to him for righteousness. **7** Know ye, therefore, that those who are of faith, they are the children of Abraham. **8** For, because God knew beforehand that the Gentiles would be made just by faith, he preannounced it to Abraham; as saith the holy scripture, In thee shall all nations be blessed. **9** Believers, therefore, it is, who are blessed with believing Abraham. **10** For they who are of the deeds of the law, are under the curse: for it is written, Cursed is every one who shall not do every thing written in this law. **11** And that no one becometh just before God, by the law, is manifest: because it is written, The just by faith, shall live. **12** Now the law is not of faith; but, whoever shall do the things written in it,	**Gal. 3:1** [1]You foolish [a]Galatians, who has bewitched you, before whose eyes Jesus Christ [b]was publicly portrayed *as* crucified? **2** This is the only thing I want to find out from you: did you receive the Spirit by the works of [1]the Law, or by [2a]hearing with faith? **3** Are you so foolish? Having begun [1]by the Spirit, are you now [2]being perfected by the flesh? **4** Did you [1]suffer so many things in vain — [a]if indeed it was in vain? **5** So then, does He who [a]provides you with the Spirit and [b]works [1]miracles among you, do it by the works of [2]the Law, or by [3a]hearing with faith?
	Gal. 3:6 [1]Even so [a]Abraham [b]BELIEVED GOD, AND IT WAS RECKONED TO HIM AS RIGHTEOUSNESS. **7** Therefore, [1]be sure that [a]it is those who are of faith who are [b]sons of Abraham. **8** The Scripture, foreseeing that God [1]would justify the [2]Gentiles by faith, preached the gospel beforehand to Abraham, *saying,* "[a]ALL THE NATIONS WILL BE BLESSED IN YOU." **9** So then [a]those who are of faith are blessed with [1]Abraham, the believer.
	Gal. 3:10 For as many as are of the works of [1]the Law are under a curse; for it is written, "[a]CURSED IS EVERYONE WHO DOES NOT ABIDE BY ALL THINGS WRITTEN IN THE BOOK

shall live by them. **13** But the Messiah hath redeemed us from the curse of the law, and hath been a curse for us; (for it is written, Cursed is everyone that is hanged on a tree;) **14** that the blessing of Abraham might be on the Gentiles, through Jesus the Messiah; that we might receive the promise of the Spirit by faith. **15** My brethren, I speak as among men; a man's covenant which is confirmed, no one setteth aside, or changeth any thing in it. **16** Now to Abraham was the promise made, and to his seed. And it said to him, not, to thy seeds, as being many; but to thy seed, as being one, which is the Messiah. **17** And this I say: That the covenant which was previously confirmed by God in the Messiah, the law which was four hundred and thirty years after, cannot set it aside, and nullify the promise. **18** And if the inheritance were by the law, it would not be by promise: but God gave it to Abraham by promise. **19** What then is the law? It was added on account of transgression, until that seed should come, to whom belonged the promise: and the law was given by angels through a mediator. **20** Now a mediator is not of one; but God is one. **21** Is the law then opposed to the promise of God? Far be it. For if a law had been given, which could make alive, certainly, righteousness would have been by the law. **22** But the scripture hath inclosed all under sin, that the promise by faith in Jesus the Messiah might be given to them that believe. **23** But before the faith came, the law kept us shut up unto the faith that was to be revealed. **24** The law, therefore, was a monitor for us unto the Messiah, that we might become just by faith. **25** But the faith having come, we are

OF THE LAW, TO PERFORM THEM." **11** Now that [a]no one is justified [1]by [2]the Law before God is evident; for, "[3b]THE RIGHTEOUS MAN SHALL LIVE BY FAITH." **12** [1]However, the Law is not [2]of faith; on the contrary, "[a]HE WHO PRACTICES THEM SHALL LIVE [3]BY THEM." **13** Christ [a]redeemed us from the curse of the Law, having become a curse for us — for it is written, "[b]CURSED IS EVERYONE WHO HANGS ON [c]A [1]TREE" — **14** in order that [a]in Christ Jesus the blessing of Abraham might [1]come to the Gentiles, so that we [b]would receive [c]the promise of the Spirit through faith.

Gal. 3:15 [a]Brethren, [b]I speak [1]in terms of human relations: [c]even though it is *only* a man's [2]covenant, yet when it has been ratified, no one sets it aside or adds [3]conditions to it. **16** Now the promises were spoken [a]to Abraham and to his seed. He does not say, "And to seeds," as *referring* to many, but *rather* to one, "[b]And to your seed," that is, Christ. **17** What I am saying is this: the Law, which came [a]four hundred and thirty years later, does not invalidate a covenant previously ratified by God, so as to nullify the promise. **18** For [a]if the inheritance is [1]based on law, it is no longer [1]based on a promise; but [b]God has granted it to Abraham by means of a promise.

Gal. 3:19 [a]Why the Law then? It was added [1]because of transgressions, having been [b]ordained through angels [c]by the [2]agency of a mediator, until [d]the seed would come to whom the promise had been made. **20** Now [a]a mediator is not [1]for one *party only;* whereas God is *only* one. **21**

not under the monitor. 26 For ye are all the children of God, by faith in Jesus the Messiah. 27 For they who have been baptized into the Messiah, have put on the Messiah. 28 There is neither Jew nor Gentile, neither slave nor free-born, neither male nor female; for ye are all one in Jesus the Messiah. 29 And if ye are the Messiah's, then are ye the seed of Abraham, and heirs by the promise.

Is the Law then contrary to the promises of God? [a]May it never be! For [b]if a law had been given which was able to impart life, then righteousness [1]would indeed have been [2]based on law. 22 But the Scripture has [a]shut up [1]everyone under sin, so that the promise by faith in Jesus Christ might be given to those who believe.

Gal. 3:23 But before faith came, we were kept in custody under the law, [a]being shut up to the faith which was later to be revealed. 24 Therefore the Law has become our [a]tutor *to lead us* to Christ, so that [b]we may be justified by faith. 25 But now that faith has come, we are no longer under a [1][a]tutor. 26 For you are all [a]sons of God through faith in [b]Christ Jesus. 27 For all of you who were [a]baptized into Christ have [b]clothed yourselves with Christ. 28 [a]There is neither Jew nor Greek, there is neither slave nor free man, there is [1]neither male nor female; for [b]you are all one in [c]Christ Jesus. 29 And if [a]you [1]belong to Christ, then you are Abraham's [2]descendants, heirs according to [b]promise.

References to the New American Standard 1995

Galatians 3:1
[1]Lit *O*
[a]Gal 1:2
[b]1 Cor 1:23; Gal 5:11

Galatians 3:2
[1]Or *law*
[2]Lit *the hearing of faith*
[a]Rom 10:17

Galatians 3:3
[1]Or *with*
[2]Or *ending with*

Galatians 3:4
[1]Or *experience*
[a]1 Cor 15:2

Galatians 3:5
[1]Or *works of power*
[2]Or *law*
[3]Lit *the hearing of faith*
[a]2 Cor 9:10; Phil 1:19
[b]1 Cor 12:10
[c]Rom 10:17

Galatians 3:6
[1]Lit *Just as*
[a]Rom 4:3
[b]Gen 15:6

Galatians 3:7
[1]Lit *know*
[a]Rom 4:16; Gal 3:9
[b]Luke 19:9; Gal 6:16

Galatians 3:8
[1]Lit *justifies*
[2]Lit *nations*

[a]Gen 12:3

Galatians 3:9

[1]Lit *the believing Abraham*
[a]Gal 3:7

Galatians 3:10

[1]Or *law*
[a]Deut 27:26

Galatians 3:11

[1]Or *in*
[2]Or *law*
[3]Or *But he who is righteous by faith shall live*
[a]Gal 2:16
[b]Hab 2:4; Rom 1:17; Heb 10:38

Galatians 3:12

[1]Or *And*
[2]Or *based on*
[3]Or *in*
[a]Lev 18:5; Rom 10:5

Galatians 3:13

[1]Or *cross;* lit *wood*
[a]Gal 4:5
[b]Deut 21:23
[c]Acts 5:30

Galatians 3:14

[1]Or *occur*
[a]Rom 4:9, 16; Gal 3:28
[b]Gal 3:2
[c]Acts 2:33; Eph 1:13

Galatians 3:15

[1]Lit *according to man*
[2]Or *will* or *testament*
[3]Or *a codicil*
[a]Acts 1:15; Rom 1:13; Gal 6:18
[b]Rom 3:5

[c]Heb 6:16

Galatians 3:16
[a]Luke 1:55; Rom 4:13, 16; 9:4
[b]Acts 3:25

Galatians 3:17
[a]Gen 15:13f; Ex 12:40; Acts 7:6

Galatians 3:18
[1]Lit *out of, from*
[a]Rom 4:14
[b]Heb 6:14

Galatians 3:19
[1]Or *for the sake of defining*
[2]Lit *hand*
[a]Rom 5:20
[b]Acts 7:53
[c]Ex 20:19; Deut 5:5
[d]Gal 3:16

Galatians 3:20
[1]Lit *of one*
[a]1 Tim 2:5; Heb 8:6; 9:15; 12:24

Galatians 3:21
[1]Or *would indeed be*
[2]Lit *out of, from*
[a]Luke 20:16; Gal 2:17
[b]Gal 2:21

Galatians 3:22
[1]Lit *things*
[a]Rom 11:32

Galatians 3:23
[a]Rom 11:32

Galatians 3:24
[a]1 Cor 4:15

[b]Gal 2:16

Galatians 3:25
[1]Lit *child-conductor*
[a]1 Cor 4:15

Galatians 3:26
[a]Rom 8:14; Gal 4:5
[b]Rom 8:1; Gal 3:28; 4:14; 5:6, 24; Eph 1:1; Phil 1:1; Col 1:4; 1 Tim 1:12; 2 Tim 1:1; Titus 1:4

Galatians 3:27
[a]Matt 28:19; Rom 6:3; 1 Cor 10:2
[b]Rom 13:14

Galatians 3:28
[1]Lit *not male and female*
[a]Rom 3:22; 1 Cor 12:13; Col 3:11
[b]John 17:11; Eph 2:15
[c]Rom 8:1; Gal 3:26; 4:14; 5:6, 24; Eph 1:1; Phil 1:1; Col 1:4; 1 Tim 1:12; 2 Tim 1:1; Titus 1:4

Galatians 3:29
[1]Lit *are Christ's*
[2]Lit *seed*
[a]Rom 4:13; 1 Cor 3:23
[b]Rom 9:8; Gal 3:18; 4:28

Koine Greek

Gal. 3:1   Ω ανοητοι Γαλαται, τις υμας εβασκανεν τη αληθεια μη πειθεσθαι, οις κατ' οφθαλμους Ιησους χριστος προεγραφη εν υμιν εσταυρωμενος; ² Τουτο μονον θελω μαθειν αφ' υμων, εξ εργων νομου το πνευμα ελαβετε, η εξ ακοης πιστεως; ³ Ουτως ανοητοι εστε; Εναρξαμενοι πνευματι, νυν σαρκι επιτελεισθε; ⁴ Τοσαυτα επαθετε εικη; ειγε και εικη. ⁵ Ο ουν επιχορηγων υμιν το πνευμα και ενεργων δυναμεις εν υμιν, εξ εργων νομου, η εξ ακοης πιστεως; ⁶ Καθως Αβρααμ επιστευσεν τω θεω, και ελογισθη αυτω εις δικαιοσυνην. ⁷ Γινωσκετε αρα οτι οι εκ πιστεως, ουτοι εισιν υιοι Αβρααμ. ⁸ Προιδουσα δε η γραφη οτι εκ πιστεως δικαιοι τα εθνη ο θεος, προευηγγελισατο τω Αβρααμ οτι Ενευλογηθησονται εν σοι παντα τα εθνη. ⁹ Ωστε οι εκ πιστεως ευλογουνται συν τω πιστω Αβρααμ. ¹⁰ Οσοι γαρ εξ εργων νομου εισιν, υπο καταραν εισιν· γεγραπται γαρ, Επικαταρατος πας ος ουκ εμμενει εν πασιν τοις γεγραμμενοις εν τω βιβλιω του νομου, του ποιησαι αυτα. ¹¹ Οτι δε εν νομω ουδεις δικαιουται παρα τω θεω, δηλον· οτι Ο δικαιος εκ πιστεως ζησεται· ¹² ο δε νομος ουκ εστιν εκ πιστεως, αλλ' Ο ποιησας αυτα ανθρωπος ζησεται εν αυτοις. ¹³ χριστος ημας εξηγορασεν εκ της καταρας του νομου, γενομενος υπερ ημων καταρα· γεγραπται γαρ Επικαταρατος πας ο κρεμαμενος επι ξυλου· ¹⁴ ινα εις τα εθνη η ευλογια του Αβρααμ γενηται εν χριστω Ιησου, ινα την επαγγελιαν του πνευματος λαβωμεν δια της πιστεως.

Gal. 3:15   Αδελφοι, κατα ανθρωπον λεγω· ομως ανθρωπου κεκυρωμενην διαθηκην ουδεις αθετει η επιδιατασσεται. ¹⁶ Τω δε Αβρααμ ερρηθησαν αι επαγγελιαι, και τω σπερματι αυτου. Ου λεγει, Και τοις σπερμασιν, ως επι πολλων, αλλ' ως εφ' ενος, Και τω σπερματι σου, ος εστιν χριστος. ¹⁷ Τουτο δε λεγω, διαθηκην προκεκυρωμενην υπο του θεου εις χριστον ο μετα ετη τετρακοσια και τριακοντα γεγονως νομος ουκ ακυροι, εις το καταργησαι την επαγγελιαν. ¹⁸ Ει γαρ εκ νομου η κληρονομια, ουκετι εξ επαγγελιας· τω δε Αβρααμ δι' επαγγελιας κεχαρισται ο θεος. ¹⁹ Τι ουν ο νομος; Των παραβασεων χαριν προσετεθη, αχρι ου ελθη το σπερμα ω επηγγελται, διαταγεις δι' αγγελων εν χειρι μεσιτου. ²⁰ Ο δε μεσιτης ενος ουκ εστιν, ο δε θεος εις εστιν. ²¹ Ο ουν νομος κατα των επαγγελιων του θεου; Μη γενοιτο. Ει γαρ εδοθη νομος ο δυναμενος ζωοποιησαι, οντως αν εκ νομου ην η δικαιοσυνη. ²² Αλλα συνεκλεισεν η γραφη τα παντα υπο αμαρτιαν, ινα η επαγγελια εκ πιστεως Ιησου χριστου δοθη τοις πιστευουσιν.

Gal. 3:23   Προ του δε ελθειν την πιστιν, υπο νομον εφρουρουμεθα, συγκεκλεισμενοι εις την μελλουσαν πιστιν αποκαλυφθηναι. ²⁴ Ωστε ο νομος παιδαγωγος ημων γεγονεν εις χριστον, ινα εκ πιστεως δικαιωθωμεν. ²⁵ Ελθουσης δε της πιστεως, ουκετι υπο παιδαγωγον εσμεν. ²⁶ Παντες γαρ υιοι θεου εστε δια της πιστεως εν χριστω Ιησου. ²⁷ Οσοι γαρ εις χριστον εβαπτισθητε, χριστον ενεδυσασθε. ²⁸ Ουκ ενι Ιουδαιος ουδε Ελλην, ουκ ενι δουλος ουδε ελευθερος, ουκ ενι αρσεν και θηλυ· παντες γαρ υμεις εις εστε εν χριστω Ιησου. ²⁹ Ει δε υμεις χριστου, αρα του Αβρααμ σπερμα εστε, και κατ' επαγγελιαν κληρονομοι.

Language

Process of Discovery

Linguistics Section

Linguistic Structure

Gal. 3:1 [1]You foolish [a]Galatians, who has bewitched you, before whose eyes Jesus Christ [b]was publicly portrayed *as* crucified? **2** This is the only thing I want to find out from you: did you receive the Spirit by the works of [1]the Law, or by [2a]hearing with faith? **3** Are you so foolish? Having begun [1]by the Spirit, are you now [2]being perfected by the flesh? **4** Did you [1]suffer so many things in vain — [a]if indeed it was in vain? **5** So then, does He who [a]provides you with the Spirit and [b]works [1]miracles among you, do it by the works of [2]the Law, or by [3]hearing with faith?

Gal. 3:6 [1]Even so [a]Abraham [b]BELIEVED GOD, AND IT WAS RECKONED TO HIM AS RIGHTEOUSNESS. **7** Therefore, [1]be sure that [a]it is those who are of faith who are [b]sons of Abraham. **8** The Scripture, foreseeing that God [1]would justify the [2]Gentiles by faith, preached the gospel beforehand to Abraham, *saying*, "[a]ALL THE NATIONS WILL BE BLESSED IN YOU." **9** So then [a]those who are of faith are blessed with [1]Abraham, the believer.

Gal. 3:10 For as many as are of the works of [1]the Law are under a curse; for it is written, "[a]CURSED IS EVERYONE WHO DOES NOT ABIDE BY ALL THINGS WRITTEN IN THE BOOK OF THE LAW, TO PERFORM THEM." **11** Now that [a]no one is justified [1]by [2]the Law before God is evident; for, "[3b]THE RIGHTEOUS MAN SHALL LIVE BY FAITH." **12** [1]However, the Law is not [2]of faith; on the contrary, "[a]HE WHO PRACTICES THEM SHALL LIVE [3]BY THEM." **13** Christ [a]redeemed us from the curse of the Law, having become a curse for us — for it is written, "[b]CURSED IS EVERYONE WHO HANGS ON [c]A [1]TREE" — **14** in order that [a]in Christ Jesus the blessing of Abraham might [1]come to the Gentiles, so that we [b]would receive [c]the promise of the Spirit through faith.

Gal. 3:15 [a]Brethren, [b]I speak [1]in terms of human relations: [c]even though it is *only* a man's [2]covenant, yet when it has been ratified, no one sets it aside or adds [3]conditions to it. **16** Now the promises were spoken [a]to Abraham and to his seed. He does not say, "And to seeds," as *referring* to many, but *rather* to one, "[b]And to your seed," that is, Christ. **17** What I am saying is this: the Law, which came [a]four hundred and thirty years later, does not invalidate a covenant previously ratified by God, so as to nullify the promise. **18** For [a]if the inheritance is [1]based on law, it is no longer [1]based on a promise; but [b]God has granted it to Abraham by means of a promise.

Gal. 3:19 [a]Why the Law then? It was added [1]because of transgressions, having been [b]ordained through angels [c]by the [2]agency of a mediator, until [d]the seed would come to whom the promise had been made. [20] Now [a]a mediator is not [1]for one *party only;* whereas God is *only* one. [21] Is the Law then contrary to the promises of God? [a]May it never be! For [b]if a law had been given which was able to impart life, then righteousness [1]would indeed have been [2]based on law. [22] But the Scripture has [a]shut up [1]everyone under sin, so that the promise by faith in Jesus Christ might be given to those who believe.

Gal. 3:23 But before faith came, we were kept in custody under the law, [a]being shut up to the faith which was later to be revealed. [24] Therefore the Law has become our [a]tutor *to lead us* to Christ, so that [b]we may be justified by faith. [25] But now that faith has come, we are no longer under a [1][a]tutor. [26] For you are all [a]sons of God through faith in [b]Christ Jesus. [27] For all of you who were [a]baptized into Christ have [b]clothed yourselves with Christ. [28] [a]There is neither Jew nor Greek, there is neither slave nor free man, there is [1]neither male nor female; for [b]you are all one in [c]Christ Jesus. [29] And if [a]you [1]belong to Christ, then you are Abraham's [2]descendants, heirs according to [b]promise.

Discussion

This chapter explains why Yeshua's death replaced the Torah.

Questioning the Passage

1. What does verse one ask?

   "O foolist Galatians, who has bewitched you" is a Semitic phrase that loses a lot of meaning in its translation to English. Opponents engage each other using every conceivable method of beguiling and deceiving one another, exactly as the serpent that beguiled Eve and induced her to break the LORD's commandments.[19]

---

[19] Rocco A. Errico and George M. Lamsa, *Aramaic Light on Galatians through Hebrews: A Commentary Based on Aramaic, the Language of Jesus, and Ancient near Eastern Customs* (Smyrna, GA: Noohra Foundation, 2005).

2. How would they know what the works of the Law was? (v. 2)

   This verse shows that this congregation was mainly a group of Jews who believed that Yeshua was the Messiah. Since they practiced the Torah Laws they certainly knew them.

3. What does verse three mean?

   This is a repeat of verse one and a bit of expansion. Apparently, the congregation abandoned the Torah Laws as Paul instructed them. Then the Jewish believers from Judea came and convinced them to reapply the Torah Laws to their lives. This verse also emphasizes Paul's completely different attitude toward the Torah. Paul knew if there were any Gentiles who came to know Yeshua as the Messiah and came to this congregation that they would probably leave because of the Torah requirement.

4. What was the suffering/events? (v. 4)

   The interpretation of this verse is notoriously difficult. It infers that evil things have happened to the congregation. First being Jewish was not an easy life in the Roman Empire. Being a Jewish-Christian congregation made matters even more difficult. Paul does not spell out what the people endured. It was probably necessary to do.

5. Who is "he" in verse five?

   This is referring to Yeshua. It was Yeshua who told his disciples to remain in Jerusalem until the Spirit was sent to them. Also, Yeshua lived among people and performed miracles.

6. Why does Paul dismiss the Torah? (v. 10-14)

Paul makes an interesting comparison between Gentiles and Abraham. Most people consider Abraham to be a Jew. He was not a Jew; he was a Gentile. There were no Jews at his time. The same can be said of Yeshua. He was not a Christian; he was a Jew. Therefore, the LORD made Abraham a patriarch of a new people who became the Hebrew people. However, since Abraham was a Gentile, the LORD said that all nations will be blessed by Abraham's faith that the LORD existed. Abraham never bowed down to idols. There are Midrash stories and legends that Abraham once broke all the idols in his father's idol store. So, Abraham was not justified before the LORD through the Torah, since the Torah had not been given yet. Therefore, the Gentiles in Paul's day must be included in the blessings of the Messiah Yeshua. Why? Because Abraham was justified and received salvation through faith in the LORD. Gentiles who come to believe in Yeshua as the Messiah must be included because of the LORD's promise to Abraham. Paul knew that many of the Laws in the Torah were written because of customs and tribal life. For example, people did not cook pork well. Numerous people died from eating undercooked pork. Therefore, a law was created that pork cannot be eaten. There are several Laws that have clear purposes for the survival of a tribe. For Paul the bottom line was that Gentiles were included in the faith of Abraham since he was a Gentile.[20]

7. What does verse thirteen mean?

Salvation comes from self-sacrifice and the power of the LORD. Moses delivered his people from the hands of the Egyptians not by a payment of a price but through much suffering, wisdom, and the mighty works of the

---

[20] IBID

LORD. The idea of Yeshua paying a ransom price for the salvation of people from sin is not a Semitic belief. Yeshua brought salvation by his suffering and death. He revealed the truth of how to free oneself from the power of sin and Satan. By following Yeshua's ways, a person stays clear of evil forces and will please the LORD. That is how one obtains salvation. The church over the centuries has taught and still teaches that Yeshua was the cosmic sacrifice for all sin. If one believes in Yeshua's acts on the cross, then one is forgiven of all sins. This is not a Semitic belief and not one that Paul was saying. Even the Sages of Israel knew the Law could not fully justify a person before the LORD because it was and is impossible to follow every Law. The Torah is a guideline of living before the LORD. It is important to live by the Laws, yet in prayer request the LORD's forgiveness for mistakes and missteps because they are going to happen. Since Yeshua came to fulfill the Torah, it is difficult to understand that Paul tosses out the Law except for the knowledge that Paul knew Gentiles would not follow the Law. The bottom line is that Yeshua suffered to bring the message that salvation and redemption comes from one trying to follow as much of the ethical parts of the Torah.

8. Why does Paul toss out the Torah, which Jesus said he came to fulfill? (v. 10-14)

Paul's attitude toward the Torah is odd, since Yeshua said that he came to fulfill the Torah. Not to be too repetitive, Paul knew that the conversion of the Mithras House churches would not have worked if he required an adherence to the Torah. Getting copies of the Torah to pass out to Gentile groups was not available in his day. The Mithras cult had several names for the deity over the centuries. Getting the Mithras church to change the name of Mithras to Yeshua and leaving almost all the cult's ways in place was easier for Paul, as history proves. The one area that Paul got the converted churches to abandon was their sexual views that were against Hebraic ethics. There are places in Paul's letters where this problem is brought up.

9. What does verse sixteen mean?

This is a very complicated verse to interpret. Since Paul quotes Genesis 15:5 the interpretation has to start there.

Genesis 15:5 And He took him outside and said, "Now look toward the heavens, and *a*count the stars, if you are able to count them." And He said to him, "*b*So shall your ¹descendants be."

⁵ וַיּוֹצֵא אֹתוֹ הַחוּצָה וַיֹּאמֶר הַבֶּט־נָא הַשָּׁמַיְמָה וּסְפֹר הַכּוֹכָבִים אִם־תּוּכַל לִסְפֹּר אֹתָם וַיֹּאמֶר לוֹ כֹּה יִהְיֶה זַרְעֶךָ׃

ךָ - this suffix is masculine singular

זַרְע this is the Hebrew word that has to be analyzed to understand Galatians 3:16. This word means "offspring." An English problem arises because offspring can be a singular and plural word. In Hebrew the ending on the word in the verse gives the interpreter the missing clue.

ךָ makes the word "one male offspring." This is what Paul used to justify verse sixteen. He interpreted this verse properly and applied it to Yeshua. Paul believed that the LORD was referring to ONE of Abraham's offspring. That ONE had to be Yeshua the Messiah. Paul also believed that Yeshua gave one teachin, andd he is the one who received it.

10. What is the significance of four hundred and thirty? (v. 17)

   This is the number of years that Abraham and his offspring were in a foreign land. The time that Abraham, Isaac, and Jacob spent in Canaan are a part of this number of years.

11. What is the significance of verse eighteen?

   Paul believed that an inheritance of salvation came from faith because it was Abraham's faith that allowed him to receive it. Abraham did not have the Torah to guide his ways, just his faith in the LORD.

12. What is verse nineteen saying?

   This verse is a direct reference to 1 Enoch, the Book of the Watchers. This book, along with Isaiah, were the most found books in Near East digs which dated from Paul's time. The people were reading and studying the Book of the Watchers. The angels were ordained by the LORD when they asked to go to the Earth. The LORD warned them they could become evil like the humans. Genesis 6:1-6 is a very short summary of the book. Evil came into the world through the angels, called the Watchers. 200 angels came to earth. Aziel, their leader, was sent to the Pit, which became Hell. The 199 other angels were condemned to the foundations of the earth. The demons described in the Gospels are some of the 199 angels who wanted to be released from their "rock" prison.

13. Is the purpose of the Law that it be used until the one offspring is born (Yeshua)? (v. 21)

Paul must now protect his readers from any Marcionite type of thinking and clarify relationships between the God-given law of Moses and the God-given promise to Abraham.[21] Marcion created an expression of Christianity in which he said that the God of the Hebrew Scriptures was not the God that Yeshua spoke. Therefore, the Hebrew Scriptures were not important nor included in his expression. Paul did not want his congregation to say, "why not be a part of Marcion's expression since Paul eliminated the Torah." To ensure that this did not happen, he told the congregation that the Torah was important to keep.

The rub here is that Marcion and his expression did not occur for another 80 years. "Marcionism was an early Christian dualistic belief system that originated with the teachings of Marcion of Sinope in Rome around the year 144 Marcion was an early Christian theologian, evangelist and an important figure in early Christianity. He was the soof a bishop of Sinope in Pontus. About the middle of the 2nd century (140–155) he traveled to Rome, where he joined the Syrian Gnostic .

Marcion preached that the benevolent God of the Gospel who sent Jesus Christ into the world as the savior was the true Supreme Being, different and opposed to the malevolent Demiurge or creator god, identified with the Hebrew God of the Old Testament. He considered himself a follower of Paul the Apostle, whom he believed to have been the only true apostle of Jesus Christ.[2][3]

---

[21] Longenecker, R. N. (1990). *Galatians* (Vol. 41, p. 143). Word, Incorporated.

Marcion's canon, possibly the first Christian canon ever compiled, consisted of eleven books: a gospel, which was a shorter version of the Gospel of Luke, and ten Pauline epistles. Marcion's canon rejected the entire Old Testament, along with all other epistles and gospels of what would become the 27-book New Testament canon, which during his life had yet to be compiled.[2][3][7][8] Pauline epistles enjoy a prominent position in the Marcionite canon, since Paul was considered by Marcion to be Christ's only true apostle.

Marcionism was denounced by its opponents as heresy and written against by the early Church Fathers – notably by Tertullian in his five-book treatise *Adversus Marcionem* (*Against Marcion*), in about 208. Marcion's writings are lost, though they were widely read and numerous manuscripts must have existed.[2][3] Even so, many scholars claim it is possible to reconstruct and deduce a large part of ancient Marcionism through what later critics, especially Tertullian, said concerning Marcion."[22]

14. Is the purpose of verse twenty-four so that the church holds onto the Hebrew Scriptures?

This was to prevent the congregation from turning to the Marcionite movement. In Paul's time, new religions had to have a basis in antiquity. Keeping the Torah, even though Paul did not want them to follow it, was important for the basis of the new religion. Since Maricon's movement does not come until 144 CE a redactor added these verses to this letter.

Comparison of citations or proof text

---

22 "Marcionism," Wikipedia (Wikimedia Foundation, April 7, 2023), https://en.wikipedia.org/wiki/Marcionism.

1. **Gal. 3:6** [1]Even so [a]Abraham [b]BELIEVED GOD, AND IT WAS RECKONED TO HIM AS RIGHTEOUSNESS.

   Genesis 15:6 And because he put his trust in the LORD, He reckoned it to his merit.

2. **Gal 3:8** The Scripture, foreseeing that God [1]would justify the [2]Gentiles by faith, preached the gospel beforehand to Abraham, *saying,* "[a]ALL THE NATIONS WILL BE BLESSED IN YOU."

   Genesis 12:3 I will bless those who bless you And curse him that curses you; And all the families of the earth Shall bless themselves by you."

3. **Gal. 3:10** For as many as are of the works of [1]the Law are under a curse; for it is written, "[a]CURSED IS EVERYONE WHO DOES NOT ABIDE BY ALL THINGS WRITTEN IN THE BOOK OF THE LAW, TO PERFORM THEM."

   Deut. 27:26 Cursed be he who will not uphold the terms of this Teaching and observe them.—And all the people shall say, Amen.

Translation Inconsistencies

1. [22] But the Scripture has [a]shut up [1]everyone under sin, so that the promise by faith **in** Jesus Christ might be given to those who believe.

   [22] Αλλα συνεκλεισεν η γραφη τα παντα υπο αμαρτιαν, ινα η επαγγελια εκ πιστεως Ιησου χριστου δοθη τοις πιστευουσιν.

Εκ – of

The bold word has the questionable translation. Is it "faith OF Yeshua" or "faith IN Yeshua." From the Greek, the proper translation is "faith of Yeshua." The English translation of the Peshitta indicates what the NASB does and that is "faith in Yeshua." The translation committees decided to incorrectly translate this verse because church tradition has said that it is the person's faith in Yeshua which gives salvation, not Yeshua's faith that the LORD would raise him in three days. Paul said that it is our faith that Yeshua had faith in the LORD that gives salvation.

Culture Section

Discussion

This congregation was probably a group of mainly Jews who believed in Paul's message that Yeshua was the Messiah promised in the Scripture. Paul's Christianity was not based on following the Torah, which is interesting since he was a Torah student all his life until he traveled on the Damascus road and meet Yeshua. The rival teachers that he spoke of were Jewish-Christians from Judea telling the congregation that believing in Yeshua as the Messiah did not mean that they had to abandon the Torah. Following the Torah was a part of the Jewish understanding about salvation. Therefore, Paul spends this entire chapter trying to convince the congregation that the Torah was nice, but is no longer necessary. Unfortunately, it is not known what Paul left in place of the Torah. In the Mithras House conversions, he left most of the Mithras practices in place. That is why 90% of Christian rituals are from the Mithras cult. Perhaps Paul was trying to get the Jewish converts to apply the Mithras' cult rituals instead of following the Torah. It mattered to Paul that these Jewish believers in the Messiah Yeshua would cling to their Torah roots. Perhaps he was concerned that they could influence his Mithras converts.

Thoughts

This is a complicated chapter that has numerous twists and turns. One thing it shows that when reading the Bible in English, there are changes in the text because of the beliefs of the church and the translation committee. This is not the only place where the English translation is clearly incorrect. Paul knew the Gentiles would not follow the Torah Laws. He also knew that it was impossible to follow everyone 100% of the time. Paul needed the conversion of Gentiles to Christians to be as simple as possible. He also could not leave Torahs with his Mithras house churches he converted, nor he could teach them Torah and continue his conversion efforts. However, the Hebrew Scriptures were important to keep in the Pauline churches because of the Marcionite movement. Paul was so self-centered that he would not share the conversion effort with anyone. Paul insisted that the Hebrews scriptures remain a part of the church which was probably not Paul's needed to be included to stop the Marcionites.

Chapter Four

Language

Peshitta	New American Standard 1995
Gal. 4:1 But I say, that the heir, so long as he is a child, differeth not from a servant, although he is lord of all; **2** but he is under supervisors and stewards, until the time established by his father. **3** So also we, while we were children, were in subordination under the elements of the world. **4** But when the consummation of the time arrived, God sent forth his Son; and he was from a woman, and was under the law; **5** that he might redeem them that were under the law; and that we might receive the adoption of sons. **6** And, because ye are sons, God hath sent forth the Spirit of his Son into your hearts, who crieth, Father, our Father. **7** Wherefore, ye are no longer servants, but sons; and if sons, then heirs of God; through Jesus the Messiah. **8** For then, when ye knew not God, ye served them who in their nature are not gods. **9** But now, since ye have known God, or rather, have been known by God, ye turn yourselves again to the weak and beggarly elements, and wish again to be under them! **10** Ye observe days and moons, and set times, and years! **11** I am afraid, lest I have labored among you in vain. **12** Be ye like me; because I have been like you. **13** My brethren, I beseech you. Ye have not injured me at all. For ye know, that under the infirmity of my flesh, I at first announced the gospel to you; **14** and the trial in my flesh, ye did not despise nor nauseate: but ye received me as an	**Gal. 4:1** Now I say, as long as the heir is a ^{1}child, he does not differ at all from a slave although he is ^{2}owner of everything, **2** but he is under guardians and ^{1}managers until the date set by the father. **3** So also we, while we were children, were held ^{a}in bondage under the ^{1b}elemental things of the world. **4** But when ^{a}the fullness of the time came, God sent forth His Son, ^{b}born of a woman, born ^{c}under ^{1}the Law, **5** so that He might redeem those who were under ^{1}the Law, that we might receive the adoption as ^{a}sons. **6** Because you are sons, ^{a}God has sent forth the Spirit of His Son into our hearts, crying, "^{b}Abba! Father!" **7** Therefore you are no longer a slave, but a son; and ^{a}if a son, then an heir ^{1}through God.
	Gal. 4:8 However at that time, ^{a}when you did not know God, you were ^{b}slaves to ^{c}those which by nature are no gods. **9** But now that you have come to know God, or rather to be ^{a}known by God, ^{b}how is it that you turn back again to the weak and worthless ^{1c}elemental things, to which you desire to be enslaved all over again? **10** You ^{a}observe days and months and seasons and years. **11** I fear for you, that perhaps I have labored ^{1}over you in vain.
	Gal. 4:12 I beg of you, ^{a}brethren, ^{b}become as I *am,* for I also *have become* as you *are.* You have done me no wrong; **13**

angel of God, and as Jesus the Messiah. **15** Where then is your blessedness? For I testify of you, that if it had been possible, ye would have plucked out your eyes, and have given them to me. **16** Have I become an enemy to you, by preaching to you the truth? **17** They are zealous towards you, yet not for good; but they wish to shut you up, that ye may be zealous towards them. **18** And it is a good thing to be zealous at all times in good things; and not merely when I am present with you. **19** [Ye are] my children, of whom I travail in birth again, till the Messiah be formed in you. **20** And I could wish to be now with you, and to change the tone of my voice; because I am astonished at you. **21** Tell me, ye who desire to be under the law, do ye not hear the law? **22** For it is written, that Abraham had two sons, one by the bondmaid, and one by the free woman. **23** But he that was by the bond maid, was born after the flesh; and he that was by the free woman, was by the promise. **24** And these are allegorical of the two covenants; the one from mount Sinai, which bringeth forth for bondage, is Hagar. **25** For Hagar is the mount Sinai in Arabia, and correspondeth with the present Jerusalem, and is serving in bondage, she and her children. **26** But the Jerusalem above, is the free woman, who is the mother of us. **27** For it is written, Be joyful, thou barren, who bearest not: exult and shout, thou who hast not travailed: for more numerous are the children of the desolate than the children of the married woman. **28** Now we, my brethren, like Isaac, are the children of the promise. **29** And as then, he that was born after the flesh, persecuted him [who was born] of the Spirit; so also [is it] now. **30** But what

but you know that it was because of a [1]bodily illness that I preached the gospel to you the [2]first time; **14** and that which was a [1]trial to you in my [2]bodily condition you did not despise or [3]loathe, but [a]you received me as an angel of God, as [b]Christ Jesus *Himself.* **15** Where then is [1]that sense of blessing you had? For I bear you witness that, if possible, you would have plucked out your eyes and given them to me. **16** So have I become your enemy [a]by [1]telling you the truth? **17** They eagerly seek you, not commendably, but they wish to shut you out so that you will seek them. **18** But it is good always to be eagerly sought in a commendable [1]manner, and [a]not only when I am present with you. **19** [a]My children, with whom [b]I am again in labor until [c]Christ is formed in you — **20** but I could wish to be present with you now and to change my tone, for [a]I am perplexed about you.

Gal. 4:21 Tell me, you who want to be under law, do you not [a]listen to the law? **22** For it is written that Abraham had two sons, [a]one by the bondwoman and [b]one by the free woman. **23** But [a]the son by the bondwoman [1]was born according to the flesh, and [b]the son by the free woman through the promise. **24** [1][a]This is allegorically speaking, for these *women* are two covenants: one *proceeding* from [b]Mount Sinai bearing children [2]who are to be [c]slaves; [3]she is Hagar. **25** Now this Hagar is Mount Sinai in Arabia and corresponds to the present Jerusalem, for she is in slavery with her children. **26** But [a]the Jerusalem above is free; [1]she is our mother. **27** For it is written,

<table>
<tr><td valign="top">

saith the scripture? Cast out the bondmaid, and her son; because the son of the bondmaid shall not inherit with the son of the free woman. [31] So then, my brethren, we are not sons of the bond-woman, but sons of the free woman.

</td><td valign="top">

"[a]REJOICE, BARREN WOMAN
WHO DOES NOT BEAR;
    BREAK FORTH AND SHOUT,
YOU WHO ARE NOT IN LABOR;
    FOR MORE NUMEROUS ARE
THE   CHILDREN   OF   THE
DESOLATE
    THAN OF THE ONE WHO HAS
A HUSBAND."
[28] And you brethren, [a]like Isaac, are [b]children of promise. [29] But as at that time [a]he who was born according to the flesh [b]persecuted him *who was born* according to the Spirit, [c]so it is now also.
[30]   But what does the Scripture say?
    "[a]CAST   OUT   THE
BONDWOMAN AND HER SON,
    FOR [b]THE   SON   OF   THE
BONDWOMAN SHALL NOT BE AN
HEIR WITH THE SON OF THE FREE
WOMAN."
[31] So then, brethren, we are not children of a bondwoman, [1]but of the free woman.

</td></tr>
</table>

References to the New American Standard 1995

Galatians 4:1
[1]Or *minor*
[2]Lit *lord*

Galatians 4:2
[1]Or *stewards*

Galatians 4:3
[1]Or *rudimentary teachings* or *principles*
[a]Gal 2:4; 4:8f, 24f
[b]Gal 4:9; Col 2:8, 20; Heb 5:12

Galatians 4:4
[1]Or *law*
[a]Mark 1:15
[b]John 1:14; Rom 1:3; 8:3; Phil 2:7
[c]Luke 2:21f, 27

Galatians 4:5
[1]Or *law*
[a]Rom 8:14; Gal 3:26

Galatians 4:6
[a]Acts 16:7; Rom 5:5; 8:9, 16; 2 Cor 3:17
[b]Mark 14:36; Rom 8:15

Galatians 4:7
[1]I.e. through the gracious act of
[a]Rom 8:17

Galatians 4:8
[a]1 Cor 1:21; Eph 2:12; 1 Thess 4:5; 2 Thess 1:8
[b]Gal 4:3
[c]2 Chr 13:9; Is 37:19; Jer 2:11; 1 Cor 8:4f; 10:20

Galatians 4:9
[1]Or *rudimentary teachings* or *principles*

[a]1 Cor 8:3
[b]Col 2:20
[c]Gal 4:3

Galatians 4:10
[a]Rom 14:5; Col 2:16

Galatians 4:11
[1]Or *for*

Galatians 4:12
[a]Gal 6:18
[b]2 Cor 6:11, 13

Galatians 4:13
[1]Lit *weakness of the flesh*
[2]Or *former*

Galatians 4:14
[1]Or *temptation*
[2]Lit *flesh*
[3]Lit *spit out at*
[a]Matt 10:40; 1 Thess 2:13
[b]Gal 3:26

Galatians 4:15
[1]Lit *the congratulation of yourselves*

Galatians 4:16
[1]Or *dealing truthfully with you*
[a]Amos 5:10

Galatians 4:18
[1]Or *thing*
[a]Gal 4:13f

Galatians 4:19
[a]1 John 2:1
[b]1 Cor 4:15
[c]Eph 4:13

Galatians 4:20
[a]2 Cor 4:8

Galatians 4:21
[a]Luke 16:29

Galatians 4:22
[a]Gen 16:15
[b]Gen 21:2

Galatians 4:23
[1]Lit *has been born*
[a]Rom 9:7; Gal 4:29
[b]Gen 17:16ff; 18:10ff; 21:1; Gal 4:28; Heb 11:11

Galatians 4:24
[1]Lit *Which*
[2]Lit *into slavery*
[3]Lit *which*
[a]1 Cor 10:11
[b]Deut 33:2
[c]Gal 4:3

Galatians 4:26
[1]Lit *which*
[a]Heb 12:22; Rev 3:12; 21:2, 10

Galatians 4:27
[a]Is 54:1

Galatians 4:28
[a]Gal 4:23
[b]Rom 9:7ff; Gal 3:29

Galatians 4:29
[a]Gal 4:23
[b]Gen 21:9
[c]Gal 5:11

Galatians 4:30
[a]Gen 21:10, 12

[b]John 8:35

Galatians 4:31
[1]V 5:1, note 1

Koine Greek

Gal. 4:1 Λεγω δε, εφ' οσον χρονον ο κληρονομος νηπιος εστιν, ουδεν διαφερει δουλου, κυριος παντων ων· ² αλλα υπο επιτροπους εστιν και οικονομους, αχρι της προθεσμιας του πατρος. ³ Ουτως και ημεις, οτε ημεν νηπιοι, υπο τα στοιχεια του κοσμου ημεν δεδουλωμενοι· ⁴ οτε δε ηλθεν το πληρωμα του χρονου, εξαπεστειλεν ο θεος τον υιον αυτου, γενομενον εκ γυναικος, γενομενον υπο νομον, ⁵ ινα τους υπο νομον εξαγοραση, ινα την υιοθεσιαν απολαβωμεν. ⁶ Οτι δε εστε υιοι, εξαπεστειλεν ο θεος το πνευμα του υιου αυτου εις τας καρδιας υμων, κραζον, Αββα, ο πατηρ. ⁷ Ωστε ουκετι ει δουλος, αλλ' υιος· ει δε υιος, και κληρονομος θεου δια χριστου.

Gal. 4:8 Αλλα τοτε μεν, ουκ ειδοτες θεον, εδουλευσατε τοις μη φυσει ουσιν θεοις· ⁹ νυν δε, γνοντες θεον, μαλλον δε γνωσθεντες υπο θεου, πως επιστρεφετε παλιν επι τα ασθενη και πτωχα στοιχεια, οις παλιν ανωθεν δουλευειν θελετε; ¹⁰ Ημερας παρατηρεισθε, και μηνας, και καιρους, και ενιαυτους. ¹¹ Φοβουμαι υμας, μηπως εικη κεκοπιακα εις υμας.

Gal. 4:12 Γινεσθε ως εγω, οτι καγω ως υμεις, αδελφοι, δεομαι υμων. Ουδεν με ηδικησατε· ¹³ οιδατε δε οτι δι' ασθενειαν της σαρκος ευηγγελισαμην υμιν το προτερον. ¹⁴ Και τον πειρασμον μου τον εν τη σαρκι μου ουκ εξουθενησατε ουδε εξεπτυσατε, αλλ' ως αγγελον θεου εδεξασθε με, ως χριστον Ιησουν. ¹⁵ Τις ουν ην ο μακαρισμος υμων; Μαρτυρω γαρ υμιν οτι, ει δυνατον, τους οφθαλμους υμων εξορυξαντες αν εδωκατε μοι. ¹⁶ Ωστε εχθρος υμων γεγονα αληθευων υμιν; ¹⁷ Ζηλουσιν υμας ου καλως, αλλα εκκλεισαι υμας θελουσιν, ινα αυτους ζηλουτε. ¹⁸ Καλον δε το ζηλουσθαι εν καλω παντοτε, και μη μονον εν τω παρειναι με προς υμας. ¹⁹ Τεκνια μου, ους παλιν ωδινω, αχρι ου μορφωθη χριστος εν υμιν, ²⁰ ηθελον δε παρειναι προς υμας αρτι, και αλλαξαι την φωνην μου, οτι απορουμαι εν υμιν.

Gal. 4:21 Λεγετε μοι, οι υπο νομον θελοντες ειναι, τον νομον ουκ ακουετε; ²² Γεγραπται γαρ, οτι Αβρααμ δυο υιους εσχεν· ενα εκ της παιδισκης, και ενα εκ της ελευθερας. ²³ Αλλ' ο μεν εκ της παιδισκης κατα σαρκα γεγεννηται, ο δε εκ της ελευθερας δια της επαγγελιας. ²⁴ Ατινα εστιν αλληγορουμενα· αυται γαρ εισιν δυο διαθηκαι· μια μεν απο ορους Σινα, εις δουλειαν γεννωσα, ητις εστιν Αγαρ. ²⁵ Το γαρ Αγαρ Σινα ορος εστιν εν τη Αραβια, συστοιχει δε τη νυν Ιερουσαλημ, δουλευει δε μετα των τεκνων αυτης. ²⁶ Η δε ανω Ιερουσαλημ ελευθερα εστιν, ητις εστιν μητηρ παντων ημων· ²⁷ γεγραπται γαρ, Ευφρανθητι στειρα η ου τικτουσα· ρηξον και βοησον η ουκ ωδινουσα· οτι πολλα τα τεκνα της ερημου μαλλον η της εχουσης τον ανδρα. ²⁸ Ημεις δε, αδελφοι, κατα Ισαακ, επαγγελιας τεκνα εσμεν. ²⁹ Αλλ' ωσπερ τοτε ο κατα σαρκα γεννηθεις εδιωκεν τον κατα πνευμα, ουτως και νυν. ³⁰ Αλλα τι λεγει η γραφη; Εκβαλε την παιδισκην και τον υιον αυτης, ου γαρ μη κληρονομηση ο υιος της παιδισκης μετα του υιου της ελευθερας. ³¹ Αρα, αδελφοι, ουκ εσμεν παιδισκης τεκνα, αλλα της ελευθερας.

Language

Process of Discovery

Linguistics Section

Linguistic Structure

[Children vs. slaves] Gal. 4:1   Now I say, as long as the heir is a [1]child, he does not differ at all from a slave although he is [2]owner of everything, **2** but he is under guardians and [1]managers until the date set by the father. **3** So also we, while we were children, were held [a]in bondage under the [1b]elemental things of the world. **4** But when [a]the fullness of the time came, God sent forth His Son, [b]born of a woman, born [c]under [1]the Law, **5** so that He might redeem those who were under [1]the Law, that we might receive the adoption as [a]sons. **6** Because you are sons, [a]God has sent forth the Spirit of His Son into our hearts, crying, "[b]Abba! Father!" **7** Therefore you are no longer a slave, but a son; and [a]if a son, then an heir [1]through God.

[Are you forgetting what Paul taught you?] Gal. 4:8   However at that time, [a]when you did not know God, you were [b]slaves to [c]those which by nature are no gods. **9** But now that you have come to know God, or rather to be [a]known by God, [b]how is it that you turn back again to the weak and worthless [1c]elemental things, to which you desire to be enslaved all over again? **10** You [a]observe days and months and seasons and years. **11** I fear for you, that perhaps I have labored [1]over you in vain.

[Why listen to Paul?] Gal. 4:12   I beg of you, [a]brethren, [b]become as I *am*, for I also *have become* as you *are*. You have done me no wrong; **13** but you know that it was because of a [1]bodily illness that I preached the gospel to you the [2]first time; **14** and that which was a [1]trial to you in my [2]bodily condition you did not despise or [3]loathe, but [a]you received me as an angel of God, as [b]Christ Jesus *Himself*. **15** Where then is [1]that sense of blessing you had? For I bear you witness that, if possible, you would have plucked out your eyes and given them to me. **16** So have I become your enemy [a]by [1]telling you the truth? **17** They eagerly seek you, not commendably, but they wish to shut you out so that you will seek them. **18** But it is good always to be eagerly sought in a commendable [1]manner, and [a]not only when I am present with you. **19** [a]My children, with whom [b]I am again in labor until [c]Christ is formed in you — **20** but I could wish to be present with you now and to change my tone, for [d]I am perplexed about you.

[Why listen to the Torah?] Gal. 4:21   Tell me, you who want to be under law, do you not [a]listen to the law? **22** For it is written that Abraham had two sons, [a]one by the bondwoman and [b]one by the free woman. **23** But [a]the son by the bondwoman [1]was born according to the flesh, and [b]the son by the free woman through the promise. **24** [1a]This is allegorically speaking, for these *women* are two covenants: one *proceeding* from [b]Mount

Sinai bearing children [2]who are to be [c]slaves; [3]she is Hagar. [25] Now this Hagar is Mount Sinai in Arabia and corresponds to the present Jerusalem, for she is in slavery with her children. [26] But [a]the Jerusalem above is free; [1]she is our mother. [27] For it is written,

"[a]REJOICE, BARREN WOMAN WHO DOES NOT BEAR;
BREAK FORTH AND SHOUT, YOU WHO ARE NOT IN LABOR;
FOR MORE NUMEROUS ARE THE CHILDREN OF THE DESOLATE
THAN OF THE ONE WHO HAS A HUSBAND."

[28] And you brethren, [a]like Isaac, are [b]children of promise. [29] But as at that time [a]he who was born according to the flesh [b]persecuted him *who was born* according to the Spirit, [c]so it is now also.

[30]   But what does the Scripture say?
"[a]CAST OUT THE BONDWOMAN AND HER SON,
FOR [b]THE SON OF THE BONDWOMAN SHALL NOT BE AN HEIR
WITH THE SON OF THE FREE WOMAN."

[31] So then, brethren, we are not children of a bondwoman, [1]but of the free woman.

Discussion

Paul continues his argument that it is unnecessary to follow the Torah to be a follower of Yeshua. Someone primarily composed this indicates that the congregation had Jewish followers.

Questioning the Passage

1. What does verse one and two mean?

Paul was constructing another argument against the Torah. He used the culture of a minor child who owns nothing and is under control of the father until a time comes when the father releases him. Usually, that time is when the child is mature and was determined by the father. Therefore, the child must obey the rules and regulations that the father establishes. This is a metaphor for the Torah and its Law. Paul believed it was put in place while Israel was "a child." The Father, Abba, decided it was time for the children to grow up. Therefore, they do not need the Law anymore. For Paul a person believing in the power of Jesus made them "a mature" person and the Law did not apply to them. Paul never defined what the ethical or moral structure was for these converts. For the Mithras Church conversions he left the ethics and morals in place except for sexual immorality (Paul's definition of what that was).

2. What are the elemental things? (v. 3)

    Paul refers to the rudimental beliefs that he gave them when he formed the congregation.

3. What does verse five mean?

    Paul said that a person does not have to be under the Law in order to receive salvation from the LORD. He believed it is only through a faith in Yeshua's ministry that allows salvation. This is a large change from his learning about the Torah.

4. What does the Spirit of his son mean? (v. 6)

    Commentators have argued whether one receives the gift of the Holy Spirit first or the Sonship first. The way the verse reads, Paul is talking about the spirit of Yeshua. The interpretation is that Paul is speaking of the two as separate entities. This expression is unique to the Galatians' letter. One can see that Paul is referring to the Spirit of the Son when reading the verse. That is Yeshua's Spirit. Here, Paul is not referring to two separate entities but one. Later on, the church will determine that there is a trinity of three, Father, Son, and Spirit. When Origen offers this explanation, then the Spirit in this verse becomes a separate entity of the triune God.

5. What did Paul believe the people were slaves to? (v. 7-9)

   Paul did not want the congregation to return to the old ways of thinking. They were returning to Torah practice. For a once Pharisee, it is difficult to image that Paul completely tossed those beliefs out in favor of the unknown practices that would eventually become the church today. He considered it going backwards to return to Jewish tradition and practices. He made this point quite clear. He added that the LORD will know the people through their faith in Yeshua's words.

6. What does verse twelve mean?

   Paul was referring to the fact that he was an avid follower of Jewish tradition and Law. He reminds the congregation that he gave up a lot to follow those traditions and law. He insists that the congregation stay the course that he had established.

7. What is the bodily condition in verse fourteen? Paul may have been suffering from a growing blindness. This is showing when he spoke about the plucking out of eyes for him. He felt that if he returned in his condition that the people would do whatever they could to help heal him.

8. What does it mean that the people received Paul as Yeshua, the Messiah? (v. 14)

   Paul would receive the honor and glory that Yeshua would have received from the people if he visited them. Paul always seemed to place himself on a higher pedestal than the average person.

9. What does verse fifteen mean?

   This verse refers to Paul knowing that if he returned in his physical condition the people would do whatever they could to help him.

10. What does verse sixteen mean?

The letter or the message to Paul must have been derogatory. Since the original questions or message sent to Paul are not available, this is a valid conclusion.

11. What does verse seventeen mean?

There might have been a group of people in the Galatians congregation who did not want Paul to return or to be heard from.

12. Why does Paul need to be with the people in order for them to be Christians? (v. 19-20)

Paul must have had a strong ego-centered personality. He wrote in several places that he was "the man."

13. What is Paul saying in verse twenty-one?

Paul returns to his arguments against the Law. It is not possible for a person to follow all the Laws in the Torah. The LORD knew this and created teshuva (repentance). Paul used the argument that the Law has no value if you cannot follow it 100% of the time in all things.

14. What does the allegory mean and to whom is it addressed? (v. 21-31)

Paul uses Isaac and Ishmael uniquely. Paul usually uses Isaac as a metaphor for the covenant between the LORD and Abraham, and views him as good. We usually view Ishmael as evil. Here Paul creates an allegory which is not necessarily in line with the usual view. He says that Hagar is bound to Mount Sinai, so she is bound to the Law, which was given to the Jewish people by the LORD at Mount Sinai. The present day, Jerusalem is the city under Roman occupation and rule. The Jerusalem above is a heavenly Jerusalem that the prophet Isaiah spoke of and verse 27 is from Isaiah 54:1. The heavenly Jerusalem is not under the Law because the Law is unnecessary in Heaven. Therefore, Paul is implying that the Peter's followers are under the Law and are slaves to it. Paul is not under the Law and since the Galatians must listen to his interpretation of Scripture and the purpose of Yeshua, then they are of the heavenly Jerusalem. They do not need the Law to be a part of the LORD's covenant with Abraham. In Romans, Paul said that the Gentiles are grafted into the covenant. This additional argument from Paul is about Gentiles being a part of the covenant.

This shows that a part of the Galatians church was Gentile. It is also possible that the original church was a Mithras church, which was converted. Then Jews from the area who believed in Yeshua as the Messiah attended the church. These Jews would have brought the Torah with them and perhaps they tried to force the Law upon the Gentiles. Since the actual questions that the letter addresses are unknown, it is speculative to determine what question Paul was addressing.

Excursus: The Hagar-Sarah Story in Jewish Writings and in Paul

"Paul was doing no injustice to the biblical text to focus attention on the contrasts and conflicts in the Hagar-Sarah story (Gen 16:1–16; 21:1–21), for those are the features on which the dynamic of the story depends. Nor was he unique in so doing. Many of the contrasts and conflicts he highlights were highlighted by other Jews as well.

The closest parallels between Paul and other Jewish writers are to be found in the materials stemming from what could be called mainline Second Temple Judaism or "formative" Judaism, both in its scholastic expressions as codified later in the Mishnah, the Palestinian and Babylonian Gemaras, the Midrashim, the Tosephta, and the numerous sayings collections of individual rabbis, and in its more popular synagogal expressions as found in the Targums. Prominent among these parallels are the many passages where a contrast is made between the slave status of Hagar and the free status of Sarah. Though late, Pirqe R. El. 30 is representative:

Rabbi Judah [the Prince] said: In that night the Holy One, blessed be He, was revealed unto him. He said to him: "Abraham! Dost thou not know that Sarah was appointed to thee for a wife from her mother's womb? She is thy companion, and the wife of thy covenant. Sarah is not called thy handmaid, but thy wife; neither is Hagar called thy wife, but thy handmaid."

The fact that Joseph was sold into slavery by the Ishmaelites (Gen 37:27) provided the basis for another comparison between the slave status of Hagar and the free status of Sarah in *Eccl. Rab.* 10.7: "I have seen servants upon horses [i.e. the Ishmaelites] and princes walking as servants [i.e. Joseph]" (Eccl 10:7). R. Levi said: A servant [i.e. Potiphar] bought him, and the sons of a handmaid sold him [i.e. the Ishmaelites], and the sons of free men were sold to both of them.

The Targums also draw attention in various ways to Hagar's slave status; for example (italics mine):

Tg. Onq. Gen 16:2 (the words of Sarah to Abraham): "Behold, now, the Lord hath restrained me from bearing; go to my handmaid and *set her free;* perhaps I may be builded by her";

Tg. *Ps.-J.* Gen 21:14 (the action of Abraham in dismissing Hagar): "And he gave [bread and a skin of water] to Hagar to bear upon her shoulders and bound [a veil] to her loins, *to signify that she was a servant*, as also the child, and dismissed her with a letter of divorce" (cf. Pirqe R. El. 30: "And he took the veil, and he bound it around her waist, so that it should drag behind her to disclose that she was a bondwoman");

Tg. Ps.-J. Gen 22:1 (the imagined dispute between Isaac and Ishmael): "And it was after these things that Isaac and Ishmael contended. Ishmael said: 'It is right that I should inherit what is the father's, because I am his first-born son.' Isaac said: 'It is right that I should inherit what is the father's, because I am the son of *Sarah his wife* and you are the son of *Hagar the handmaid* of my mother.' "

Though charges of idolatry and wickedness are often leveled in the rabbinic writings against Ishmael, the situation is more ambivalent with regard to Hagar. In an attempt to justify Sarah's treatment of Hagar, especially since it was Sarah who first suggested Abraham's sexual involvement with her, the Targums and early Midrashim claim that Hagar was the granddaughter of the impious King Nimrod who threw Abraham into the fiery furnace after Abraham destroyed his idols (cf. *Tg. Ps.-J.* Gen 16:1, 5; *Tg. Neof.* Gen 16:5; Frg. Tg. Gen 16:5; *Gen. Rab.* 45.1; see L. Ginzberg, *The Legends of the Jews*, tr. H. Szold [Philadelphia: Jewish Publication Society, 1937] 1:198–203). In a similar vein, *Gen. Rab.* 45.4 has it that Hagar told certain solicitous ladies that had Sarah been a righteous woman, she would have had no trouble conceiving. And in Pirqe R. El. 30 Hagar's expulsion by Abraham is justified on the basis of her idolatrous tendencies:

By the merit of our father Abraham, the water did not fail in the bottle. But when she reached the entrance to the wilderness she began to go astray after the idolatry of her father's house, and forthwith the water in the bottle was spent.

But such accusations against Hagar are not common in the rabbinic materials. Usually she is elevated to the status of a daughter of Pharoah who was given by her father to Abraham as a servant in recompense for attempting to take Sarah into his harem and in acknowledgment of God's presence with Abraham (Gen 12:10–20), for, said Pharaoh, "Better let my daughter be a handmaid in this house than a mistress in another house" (*Gen. Rab.* 45.1; cf. *Tg. Ps.-J.* Gen 16:1; Pirqe R. El. 26).

Charges of idolatry and wickedness, however, are frequently leveled against Ishmael, often in explicit contrast to Isaac and, of course, with an implied polemic against the Arabs vis-à-vis the Jews. So, for example, when dealing with the question of why Abraham did not bless his children when God allowed him to bless whom he would (cf. Gen 12:2), *Num. Rab.* 11.2 reads:

Nevertheless Abraham did not bless his children. Why was this? It may be illustrated by the parable of a king who possessed an orchard which he gave over to a tenant. Now in that orchard there was one tree which yielded a life-giving potion and another which yielded deadly poison. Said the tenant: "I shall just cultivate it and accomplish my task. Let the king do whatever he likes with his orchard." So here the king is the Holy One, blessed be He, and the orchard is the world. He handed it over to Abraham by saying to him: "Be thou a blessing." What did Abraham do? He had two sons, one righteous and one wicked, Isaac and Ishmael. Abraham thought: "If I bless Isaac, then Ishmael will wish to be blessed, and he is wicked. But I am God's servant; I am flesh and blood, and will be gone from this world tomorrow. Let the Holy One, blessed be He, do with this world of His as He pleases. When Abraham died, the Holy One, blessed be He, revealed Himself to Isaac and blessed him.

Likewise, when attempting to justify Abraham's expulsion of Hagar and Ishmael—which, on the face of it, appears to be a very callous act—the rabbis pointed to Ishmael's idolatry, wickedness, and mistreatment of Isaac as necessitating it, as in ExodRab 1.1:

Then why: "He that spareth his rod hateth his son"? To teach you that anyone who refrains from chastising his son causes him to fall into evil ways and so comes to hate him. This is what we find in the case of Ishmael, who behaved wickedly before Abraham his father; but he did not chastise him, with the result that he fell into evil ways so that he despised him and cast him forth empty-handed from his house. What did Ishmael do? When he was fifteen years old, he commenced to bring idols from the street, toyed with them as he had seen others do. So "when Sarah saw the son of Hagar the Egyptian, whom she had borne unto Abraham, making sport" (Gen 21:9) [מצחק (*mĕṣaḥēq*), "making sport," here understood as idolatrous worship], she immediately "said unto Abraham: 'Cast out this bondwoman and her son' (Gen 21:10) lest my son learn of his ways." Hence "and the thing was very grievous in Abraham's sight on account of his son" (Gen 21:11), because he had become depraved.... He hated Ishmael because of his evil ways and sent him together with his mother Hagar away empty-handed and expelled him from his house on this account. [For otherwise] do you really think that Abraham, of whom it is written: "And Abraham was very rich in cattle" (Gen 13:2), could send away his wife and son from his house empty-handed without clothes or means of livelihood? But this is to teach you that when Ishmael became depraved he ceased to think about him. What became of him in the end? After he had driven him out, he sat at the cross-roads and robbed and molested passers-by, as it is said: "And he shall be a wild ass of a man: his hand shall be against every man" (Gen 16:12).

So Ishmael is characterized in the literature of "formative" Judaism as "doing evil works" by being involved in "strange worship" (cf. *Tg. Ps.-J.*, Tg. Onq., *Tg. Neof.*, and Frg. Tg. on Gen 21:9) and as persecuting his younger brother Isaac, often by "shooting deadly arrows at him" when out hunting birds (cf. *Pesiq. R.* 48.2; Pirqe R. El. 30). And to these passages that speak of Ishmael's wickedness, numerous others can be added (e.g., *Gen. Rab.* 53.4; 62.5; *Exod. Rab.* 3.2; DeutRab 4.5).

In fact, Ishmael and Esau are viewed in the rabbinic writings as wicked anomalies in an otherwise righteous line. The Babylonian Gemara Pesaḥ. 119b pictures Abraham at the banquet for the righteous refusing to take the cup of grace offered him and saying: "I cannot say Grace, because Ishmael issued from me." And this lament regarding Ishmael, together with Esau, appears a number of times in the writings of the rabbis; for example:

*b.*Pesaḥ. 56a (credited to Rabbi Simeon ben Lakish): "Perhaps, heaven forbid, there is one unfit among my children, like Abraham from whom there issued Ishmael, or like my father Isaac, from whom there issued Esau."

b.Šabb. 146a (credited to Rabbi Aliba ben Kahana): "Until three generations the lustful [strain] did not disappear from our Patriarchs: Abraham begat Ishmael, Isaac begat Esau, [but] Jacob begat the twelve tribes in whom there was no taint whatsoever."

Lev. Rab. 36.5: "From Abraham sprang Ishmael and all the sons of Keturah; from Isaac sprang Esau and all the chiefs of Edom; but Jacob's bed was perfect, all his sons being righteous."

Num. Rab. 2.13 (answering the question, Why are the righteous in Dan 12:3 compared to the stars rather than to the sun or moon?): "For this reason: Abraham was compared to the sun, Isaac to the moon, and Jacob to the stars.

In the Messianic era the sun and moon will suffer humiliation, as it is said 'the moon will be abashed, the sun ashamed' [Isa 24:23]. The stars, however, will not be humiliated. Thus it will be with Abraham and Isaac, whose faces in the hereafter will blanch on account of their children: Abraham's because of Ishmael and the sons of Keturah; Isaac's on account of Esau and his chiefs. And as the stars will suffer no humiliation, so also will Jacob suffer no humiliation, for he will not need to feel shame [all his children being righteous]."

The story of the ʿAqēdâ Isaac ("Binding of Isaac") also became an occasion to draw contrasts between Isaac and Ishmael. It was, in fact, a discussion between Isaac and Ishmael over their comparative degrees of righteousness that was seen by some rabbis to have been the occasion for the ʿAqēdâ in the first place. Two passages, one from a Babylonian Gemara and one from the Targums, are particularly significant here and deserve to be quoted in full:

*b.*Sanh. 89b (credited to Rabbi Levi): "Ishmael said to Isaac: 'I am more righteous than you in good deeds, for you were circumcised at eight days [and so could not prevent your circumcision], but I at thirteen years [and so accepted circumcision willingly].' 'On account of one limb would you incense me?,' he [Isaac] replied. 'Were the Holy One, blessed be He, to say unto me: "Sacrifice yourself before me," I would obey.' Straightway, 'God did tempt Abraham' (Gen 22:1)";

Tg. Ps.-J. Gen 22:1 (the first part of which has been cited above with regard to the contrast between Hagar and Sarah): "And it was after these things that Isaac and Ishmael contended. Ishmael said: 'It is right that I should inherit what is the father's', because I am his first-born son.' Isaac said: 'It is right that I should inherit what is the father's', because I am the son of Sarah his wife, and you are the son of Hagar the handmaid of my mother.' Ishmael answered and said: 'I am more righteous than you, because I was circumcised at thirteen years; and if it had been my will to hinder, they should not have delivered me to be circumcised. But you were circumcised a child of eight days; if you had knowledge perhaps they could not have delivered you to be circumcised.' Isaac responded and said: 'Behold now, today I am thirty and six years old; and if the Holy One, blessed be He, were to require all my members, I would not delay.' These words were heard before the Lord of the universe, and immediately, the word of the Lord tested Abraham, and said to him, 'Abraham,' and he said, 'Here am I.' "

Similar contrasts between Ishmael and Isaac appear further on in the *Aqēdâ* Isaac story. In rabbinic tradition it was believed that the two young men who accompanied Abraham and Isaac on their journey to Mt. Moriah (Gen 22:3) were none other than Ishmael and Eliezer (cf. *Tg. Ps.-J.* Gen 22:3; *Lev. Rab.* 26.7). When they approached Mt. Moriah, its peak was enveloped in a cloud that was visible to Abraham and Isaac but not to Ishmael and Eliezer (cf. *Lev. Rab.* 20.2; *Eccl. Rab.* 9.7; Pirqe R. El. 31). Pirqe R. El. 31 even adds that when Isaac was about to be offered, Ishmael and Eliezer engaged in the following shameless dispute:

Ishmael said to Eliezer: "Now that Abraham will offer Isaac his son for a burnt offering, kindled upon the altar, and I am his firstborn son, I will inherit [the possessions of] Abraham." Eliezer replied to him, saying: "He has already driven you out like a woman divorced from her husband, and he has sent you away to the wilderness, but I am his servant, serving him by day and by night, and I shall be the heir of Abraham." The Holy Spirit answered them, saying to them: "Neither this one nor that one shall inherit."

There is, however, no way of determining just how much of this rabbinic tradition regarding Hagar and Ishmael had been developed by Paul's day, though the Targumic elaborations suggest that at least some of it had. Furthermore, given the fact that the contrasts in the story are readily apparent to any reader, similarities between Paul and the rabbis do not necessarily imply either familiarity or dependence. Still, it is useful to note that interest in the contrast of status between Hagar and Sarah and the contrast of righteousness between Ishmael and Isaac was not unique to Paul, and it is possible to speculate that in these matters Paul was dipping into certain streams of tradition that were already flowing within Judaism, possibly even into a stream of tradition that was being used against him by his judaizing opponents at Galatia.

Yet Paul was not interested in the contrasts of the Hagar-Sarah story for their own sakes. Rather, he used them in what appears to be an ad hominem fashion in his exhortations to his Galatian converts against what they had heard from the Judaizers—that is, to align the negative side of the contrasts with his judaizing opponents. This raises the question of whether there are any parallels in Jewish tradition to the way in which Paul uses this story in Gal 4:21–31: How was it "contemporized" in the Judaism of Paul's day? The most extensive utilization of the Hagar-Sarah story for contemporary purposes, of course, is to be found in the writings of Philo. Like other Jewish commentators, Philo was drawn to the contrasts of slave and free and the conflicts that resulted in the banishment of Hagar and Ishmael. His own allegorical interpretation of the story, however, depends on a further observation: that Abraham was able to be fruitful with Sarah only after he had first produced offspring with Hagar.

For Philo, Hagar the handmaid symbolizes the preliminary learning that can be obtained in the schools, that is, "grammar, geometry, astronomy, rhetoric, music, and all the other branches of intellectual study" (*Congr.* 11)—with the fruit of the mating of the mind with this "lower instruction" being sophistry (*Congr.* 12), or producing a man like Ishmael "with his pretense of excessive openmindedness and his love of arguing for arguing's sake" (*Fug.* 209). Sarah, the mistress of the house, on the other hand, exemplifies virtue, and her offspring is true wisdom. Just as Hagar conceived before Sarah, so the search for wisdom must begin with the "lower branches of school lore"; but just as Hagar was expelled at the command of Sarah, so it is necessary to move beyond mere sophistry and mundane learning if one wishes to attain wisdom and virtue. The Hagar-Sarah story provides for Philo, in fact, the basis for an entire allegorical treatise, "On Mating with the Preliminary Studies" (*De Congressu Eruditionis Gratia*), and is a recurring feature in Philo's writings (cf. esp. *Cher.* 3–10; *Poster* 130–31; *Mutat.* 261; *Somn.* 1.240; *Fug.* 209–13; *Sacrif.* 43–44; *Quaest. Gen.* 3.19–35). The following is a representative sample of such passages:

Congr. 9–10: "For we are not capable as yet of receiving the impregnation of virtue unless we have first mated with her handmaiden, and the handmaiden of wisdom is the culture gained by the primary learning of the school course. For, just as in houses we have outer doors in front of the chamber doors, and in cities suburbs through which we can pass to the inner part, so the school course precedes virtue; the one is a road which leads to the other";

Congr. 12: "What is meant [by Abraham's unions with Hagar and Sarah] is a mating of mind with virtue. Mind desires to have children by virtue, and, if it cannot do so at once, is instructed to espouse virtue's handmaid, the lower instruction";

Congr. 14: " 'Go in, then,' she says, 'to my handmaid, the lower instruction given by the lower branches of school lore, that first you may have children by her,' for afterwards you will be able to avail yourself of the mistress's company to beget children of higher birth";

Congr. 23: "Sarah, virtue, bears, we shall find, the same relation to Hagar, education, as the mistress to the servant-maid, or the lawful wife to the concubine, and so naturally the mind which aspires to study and to gain knowledge, the mind we call Abraham, will have Sarah, virtue, for his wife, and Hagar, the whole range of school culture, for his concubine";

Cher. 9: "When all this is come to pass [i.e., the name changes that mean that Abraham and Sarah have achieved true wisdom], then will be cast forth those preliminary studies which bear the name of Hagar, and cast forth too will be their son the sophist named Ishmael";

Leg. All. 3.244: "The wise Abraham complies with her [Sarah/virtue] when she recommends the course to follow. For at an earlier time, when he had not yet become perfect but, before his name had been changed, was still only inquiring into supramundane things, being aware that he could not beget seed out of perfect virtue, she advises him to beget children out of the handmaiden, that is school-learning, even Hagar. This name means 'Sojourning,' for he that is studying to make his home in perfect virtue, before he is registered as a member of her city, sojourns with the subjects learned in the schools, that he may be lead by these to apply his unfettered powers to virtue";

Quaest. Gen. 3.1: " 'Hagar' is interpreted as 'sojourning' and she is a servant, waiting on a more perfect nature. And she is very naturally an Egyptian by race. For she is the study of school disciplines, and being a lover of wide learning, is in a certain sense a servant waiting on virtue, since school studies are serviceable to him who needs help in receiving it, inasmuch as virtue has the soul as its place, while the school studies need bodily organs; and Egypt is symbolically the body, (wherefore Scripture) rightly describes the form of the school studies as Egyptian. Moreover, it also named her 'sojourning' for the reason that sophistry is a sojourner in comparison with native virtue which alone is at home and which is mistress of intermediate education and provides for us through the school studies" (*Philo I–X*, ed. F. H. Colson et al. [LCL; London: Heinemann, 1929–62]).

Philo's Hagar-Sarah allegory bears several striking surface similarities to Paul's in Gal 4:21–31. Both depend on similar elements in the story: the contrast between slave and free; the two sons; the banishment of Hagar and Ishmael in favor of Sarah and Isaac. In both, Hagar and Ishmael represent a preliminary and preparatory stage that is superseded by something greater, rather than a totally negative and wicked quantity as is the case in rabbinic tradition. Yet these similarities may have arisen quite naturally from the Genesis account itself and demonstrate nothing more than that Paul and Philo both read Scripture. Apart from their desire to contemporize the story and certain surface similarities, the allegorical interpretations of Paul and Philo are sufficiently divergent to suggest independence.

When one looks into the rabbinic traditions for a similar contemporization of the Hagar-Sarah story in which the interpreter's opponents are identified with Hagar and Ishmael and so denounced or marginalized, one finds the potential but not the reality—that is, one finds all the elements being present, but not, with only rare and generally late exceptions, being brought together for polemical purposes.

There was, of course, as noted above, an extant rabbinic tradition that drew from the Ishmael and Esau stories the theological conclusion that the salvation-historical line did not include all of Abraham's offspring. Particularly quotable here is *Pesiq. R.* 48.2:

The Holy One, blessed be He, says: "I always love the pursued and hate the pursuers, as when Ishmael pursued his brother Isaac"—"And Sarah saw the son of Hagar the Egyptian … making sport" [Gen 21:9]. Because Ishmael shot arrows at Isaac—"As one who makes sport by shooting deadly arrows, and said, Am not I in sport?" [Prov 26:18–19]—the Holy One, blessed be He, loved Isaac, saying to Abraham: "Take now thy son" [Gen 22:2]. Our father Abraham replied: "I have two sons; Thou hast given me Isaac and Ishmael." God said: "Thine only son." Abraham replied: "Both are only sons; Isaac is an only son to Sarah and Ishmael an only son to Hagar." God said: "Whom thou lovest." Abraham replied: "Are there different areas of love within a man—one of more love for one son and of less love for the other? I love both of them." God declared: "Even Isaac—for it is Isaac I love because he is pursued" (cf. also *b.Ned.* 31a *Gen. Rab.* 55.7; *Deut. Rab.* 4.5).

Ishmael was frequently identified with various non-Jewish groups, particularly the Arabs (e.g., *Pesiq. R.* 21.2–3; Pirqe R. El. 41; *Lam. Rab.* 3.1; cf. also *Jub.* 20:13; Josephus, *Ant.* 1.221), sometimes Gentiles generally (e.g., *Gen. Rab.* 45.8), and once or twice a foreign king (e.g., Nebuchadnezzar in *Exod. Rab.* 27.1). But most of these identifications of Ishmael with the Arabs, the Gentiles, or a foreign ruler are stated in a more or less matter-of-fact manner, with no explicit polemical or contemporizing edge to them (though possibly such should be seen as implied).

Closer parallels to Paul's contemporization in Gal 4:21–31, however, can be seen in the Qumran *War Scroll*, where in 1QM 2.13 the battle plans for the ninth year include an attack on "the descendants of Ishmael and Keturah," for here Ishmael is seen as one of the progenitors of the "Sons of Darkness." Likewise in *Gen. Rab.* 45.9, in a discussion of the phrases "he shall dwell" (Gen 16:12) and "he fell" (Gen 25:17), Ishmael seems to be identified either with Aretas, the king of Nabatea who attacked Aristobulus and besieged Jerusalem (cf. Josephus, *Ant.* 14.19–21), or with the Arabian prince who joined Vespasian's army in the siege and destruction of Jerusalem, and so read from the perspective of a contemporary situation of opposition. As well, Pirqe R. El. 30 and 32 speak of "the children of Ishmael" (Arabs? Gentiles?) bringing about oppression in the land in the last days, for which reason, it is said, Hagar's son was called Ishmael. Going beyond the confines of the Hagar-Sarah story itself, there are numerous parallels to Paul's contemporizing of Scripture in various Jewish writings. The targumic interpretations of the Cain and Abel story of Gen 4, for example, which view the dispute that led to that fatal confrontation as being over the doctrine of the resurrection, obviously have the Sadducees in mind when depicting the nefarious figure of Cain. And Scripture is handled in similar fashion at Qumran, particularly in the treatment of Hab 2:17 in 1QpHab 12.3–4 where "Lebanon" (etymologically "white") stands for the Communal Council (who dressed in white) and "wild beasts" for the simple minded Jews who carry out the law, as well as in the treatment of Num 21:8 ("The Song of the Well") in CD 6.3–11 where "well" stands for the law, the "princes" who dig it for the members of the community, the "sceptre" or "staff" with which it is dug for "the expositor of the law," and "the nobles of the people" for those who carry out his ordinances (cf. 1QpMic 8–10 and CD 7.9–20 for other allegorical contemporizations).

With respect to the specific Hagar-Sarah story, though there is enough interest in the contrasts and conflicts of the story in Jewish writings to suggest that Paul's use of it was not entirely unique, there is no evidence that his particular allegorical treatment of it was following any Jewish prototype, particularly in the identification he makes between Hagar, Ishmael, Mt. Sinai, and the present city of Jerusalem, and in the contrast he sets out between "the Jerusalem that is above" vis-à-vis Mt. Sinai and the present city of Jerusalem. To understand Paul's Hagar-Sarah allegory, therefore, it seems that at least four factors must be taken into account: (1) Paul's Jewish heritage, which was not averse to highlighting the contrasts and conflicts of the story; (2) tendencies within the various streams of Judaism generally to contemporize the persons and places of the biblical narrative for their own purposes, whether such contemporizations be understood as allegorical or typological treatments; (3) the Judaizers' contemporization of the story, with the polemics of their usage probably directed against Paul; and (4) Paul's own ad hominem use, with his polemics directed against the Judaizers."[23]

Verse Comparison of citations or proof text

1. [4:7] For it is written,

    "'REJOICE, BARREN WOMAN WHO DOES NOT BEAR; BREAK FORTH AND SHOUT, YOU WHO ARE NOT IN LABOR; FOR MORE NUMEROUS ARE THE CHILDREN OF THE DESOLATE THAN OF THE ONE WHO HAS A HUSBAND."

---

[23] Longenecker, R. N. (1990). *Galatians* (Vol. 41, pp. 200–206). Word, Incorporated.

Is. 54:1   "*ᵃ*Shout for joy, O barren one, you who have borne no *child;* Break forth into joyful shouting and cry aloud, you who have not travailed; For the sons of the *ᵇ*desolate one *will be* *ᶜ*more numerous than the sons of the married woman," says the LORD.

2. **³⁰** But what does the Scripture say? "*ᵃ*CAST OUT THE BONDWOMAN AND HER SON, FOR *ᵇ*THE SON OF THE BONDWOMAN SHALL NOT BE AN HEIR WITH THE SON OF THE FREE WOMAN."

Genesis 21:10 Therefore she said to Abraham, "*ᵃ*Drive out this maid and her son, for the son of this maid shall not be an heir with my son ¹Isaac."

Phrase Study

1. υιοθεσια, ας, η (v. 5) "***adoption,*** lit. a legal t.t. of 'adoption' of children, in our lit., i.e. in Paul, only in a transferred sense of a transcendent filial relationship between God and humans (with the legal aspect, not gender specificity, as major semantic component)

a. of the acceptance of the nation of Israel as son of God. **Gal 4:5**; cp. Eph 1:5. η δι αυτου διδομενη υιοθεσια AcPl Ha 2, 28 (s. app.). The Spirit, whom the converts receive, works as πνευμα υιοθεσιας Ro 8:15 (opp. πν. δουλειας=such a spirit as is possessed by a slave, not by the son of the house). The believers enter into full enjoyment of their υιοθεσια only when the time of fulfillment releases them from the earthly body."[24]

---

[24] Frederick W. Danker and Bernard A. Taylor, *Biblical Greek Language and Lexicography: Essays in Honor of Frederick W. Danker* (Grand Rapids, MI: Wm. B. Eerdmans, 2004).

Thoughts

It is amazing how Paul went through this transition of being a devout Torah follower to becoming completely against it. His mission to evangelize for the Yeshua movement and releasing the Torah allowed him to convert Gentiles. Paul refused to accept the burdens of Jewish tradition and Law. In the cases of Jewish converts, the idea of removing all the Law and traditions was a sticking point. When a congregation became mixed Jews and Gentiles, Paul had trouble because some Jews did not want to leave everything behind. This chapter is another version of Paul's argument to abandon Torah teachings. For the Jewish converts, Paul did not have a new book of ethics and morals. For the Mithras converts, he told them to continue living as they did with the removal of the sexual indiscretions.

Chapter Five

Language

Peshitta	New American Standard 1995
Gal. 5:1 Stand fast, therefore, in the liberty with which the Messiah hath made us free; and be not subjected again to the yoke of bondage. **2** Behold, I Paul say to you, That if ye become circumcised, the Messiah is of no advantage to you. **3** And again, I testify to every one who becometh circumcised, that he is bound to fulfill the whole law. **4** Ye have renounced the Messiah, ye who seek justification by the law: and ye have apostatized from grace. **5** For we, through the Spirit, which is from faith, are waiting for the hope of righteousness. **6** For, in the Messiah Jesus, circumcision is nothing, neither is uncircumcision, but the faith that is perfected by love. **7** Ye did run well: who hath interrupted you, that ye acquiesce not in the truth? **8** The bias of your mind is not from him who called you. **9** A little leaven leaveneth the whole mass. **10** I confide in you through our Lord, that ye will entertain no other thoughts. And he that disquieteth you, shall bear his judgment, whoever he may be. **11** And I, my brethren, if I still preached circumcision, why should I suffer persecution? Hath the offensiveness of the cross ceased? **12** But I would, that they who disquiet you, were actually cut off. **13** And ye, my brethren, have been called into liberty: only let not your liberty be an occasion to the flesh; but, by love, be ye servants to each other. **14** For the whole law is fulfilled in one	**Gal. 5:1** [1a]It was for freedom that Christ set us free; therefore [b]keep standing firm and do not be subject again to a [c]yoke of slavery. **Gal. 5:2** Behold I, [a]Paul, say to you that if you receive [b]circumcision, Christ will be of no benefit to you. **3** And I [a]testify again to every man who receives [b]circumcision, that he is under obligation to [c]keep the whole Law. **4** You have been severed from Christ, you who [1]are seeking to be justified by law; you have [a]fallen from grace. **5** For we [1]through the Spirit, [2]by faith, are [a]waiting for the hope of righteousness. **6** For in [a]Christ Jesus [b]neither circumcision nor uncircumcision means anything, but [c]faith working through love. **Gal. 5:7** You were [a]running well; who hindered you from obeying the truth? **8** This persuasion *did* not *come* from [a]Him who calls you. **9** [a]A little leaven leavens the whole lump *of dough.* **10** [a]I have confidence [1]in you in the Lord that you [b]will adopt no other view; but the one who is [c]disturbing you will bear his judgment, whoever he is. **11** But I, brethren, if I still preach circumcision, why am I still [a]persecuted? Then [b]the stumbling block of the cross has been abolished. **12** I wish that [a]those who are troubling you would even [1b]mutilate themselves.

sentence; in this, Thou shalt love thy neighbor as thyself. **15** But if ye bite and devour one another, beware, lest ye be consumed one by another. **16** And I say: Walk ye in the Spirit; and never follow the cravings of the flesh. **17** For the flesh craveth that which is repugnant to the Spirit; and the Spirit craveth that which is repugnant to the flesh: and the two are the opposites of each other, so that ye do not that which ye desire. **18** But if ye are guided by the Spirit, ye are not under the law. **19** For the works of the flesh are known, which are whoredom, impurity, lasciviousness, **20** idol-worship, magic, malice, contention, rivalry, wrath, strife, divisions, discords, **21** envy, murder, drunkenness, revelling, and all the like things. And they who perpetrate these things, as I have before told you, and also now tell you, do not inherit the kingdom of God. **22** But the fruits of the Spirit are, love, joy, peace, long suffering, suavity, kindness, fidelity, modesty, patience. **23** Against these there standeth no law. **24** And they who are of the Messiah, have crucified their flesh, with all its passions and its cravings. **25** Let us therefore live in the Spirit; and let us press on after the Spirit. **26** And let us not be vain-glorious, despising one another, and envying one another.

Gal. 5:13 For you were called to *a*freedom, brethren; *b*only *do* not *turn* your freedom into an opportunity for the flesh, but through love *c*serve one another. **14** For *a*the whole Law is fulfilled in one word, in the *statement,* "*b*YOU SHALL LOVE YOUR NEIGHBOR AS YOURSELF." **15** But if you *a*bite and devour one another, take care that you are not consumed by one another.

Gal. 5:16 But I say, *a*walk by the Spirit, and you will not carry out *b*the desire of the flesh. **17** For *a*the flesh [1]sets its desire against the Spirit, and the Spirit against the flesh; for these are in opposition to one another, *b*so that you may not do the things that you [2]please. **18** But if you are *a*led by the Spirit, *b*you are not under the Law. **19** Now the deeds of the flesh are evident, which are: [1*a*]immorality, impurity, sensuality, **20** idolatry, *a*sorcery, enmities, *b*strife, jealousy, outbursts of anger, *c*disputes, dissensions, [1*d*]factions, **21** envying, *a*drunkenness, carousing, and things like these, of which I forewarn you, just as I have forewarned you, that those who practice such things will not *b*inherit the kingdom of God. **22** But *a*the fruit of the Spirit is *b*love, joy, peace, patience, kindness, goodness, faithfulness, **23** gentleness, *a*self-control; against such things *b*there is no law. **24** Now those who [1]belong to *a*Christ Jesus have *b*crucified the flesh with its passions and *c*desires.

Gal. 5:25 If we live by the Spirit, let us also [1]walk *a*by the Spirit. **26** Let us not become *a*boastful, challenging one another, envying one another.

References to the New American Standard 1995

Galatians 5:1

[1]Some authorities prefer to join with 4:31 and render *but with the freedom of the free woman Christ set us free*

[a]John 8:32, 36; Rom 8:15; 2 Cor 3:17; Gal 2:4; 5:13

[b]1 Cor 16:13

[c]Acts 15:10; Gal 2:4

Galatians 5:2

[a]2 Cor 10:1

[b]Acts 15:1; Gal 5:3, 6, 11

Galatians 5:3

[a]Luke 16:28

[b]Acts 15:1; Gal 5:2, 6, 11

[c]Rom 2:25

Galatians 5:4

[1]Or *would be*

[a]Heb 12:15; 2 Pet 3:17

Galatians 5:5

[1]Lit *by*

[2]Lit *out of*

[a]Rom 8:23; 1 Cor 1:7

Galatians 5:6

[a]Gal 3:26

[b]1 Cor 7:19; Gal 6:15

[c]Col 1:4f; 1 Thess 1:3; James 2:18, 20, 22

Galatians 5:7

[a]Gal 2:2

Galatians 5:8

[a]Rom 8:28; Gal 1:6

Galatians 5:9
[a]1 Cor 5:6

Galatians 5:10
[1]Lit *toward*
[a]2 Cor 2:3
[b]Gal 5:7; Phil 3:15
[c]Gal 1:7; 5:12

Galatians 5:11
[a]Gal 4:29; 6:12
[b]Rom 9:33; 1 Cor 1:23

Galatians 5:12
[1]Or *cut themselves off*
[a]Gal 2:4; 5:10
[b]Deut 23:1

Galatians 5:13
[a]Gal 5:1
[b]1 Cor 8:9; 1 Pet 2:16
[c]1 Cor 9:19; Eph 5:21

Galatians 5:14
[a]Matt 7:12; 22:40; Rom 13:8, 10; Gal 6:2
[b]Lev 19:18; Matt 19:19; John 13:34

Galatians 5:15
[a]Gal 5:20; Phil 3:2

Galatians 5:16
[a]Rom 8:4; 13:14; Gal 5:24f
[b]Rom 13:14; Eph 2:3

Galatians 5:17
[1]Lit *lusts against*
[2]Lit *wish*
[a]Rom 7:18, 23; 8:5ff
[b]Rom 7:15ff

Galatians 5:18
[a]Rom 8:14
[b]Rom 6:14; 7:4; 1 Tim 1:9

Galatians 5:19
[1]I.e. sexual immorality
[a]1 Cor 6:9, 18; 2 Cor 12:21

Galatians 5:20
[1]Or *heresies*
[a]Rev 21:8
[b]2 Cor 12:20
[c]Rom 2:8; James 3:14ff
[d]1 Cor 11:19

Galatians 5:21
[a]Rom 13:13
[b]1 Cor 6:9

Galatians 5:22
[a]Matt 7:16ff; Eph 5:9
[b]Rom 5:1-5; 1 Cor 13:4; Col 3:12-15

Galatians 5:23
[a]Acts 24:25
[b]Gal 5:18

Galatians 5:24
[1]Lit *are of Christ Jesus*
[a]Gal 3:26
[b]Rom 6:6; Gal 2:20; 6:14
[c]Gal 5:16f

Galatians 5:25
[1]Or *follow the Spirit*
[a]Gal 5:16

Galatians 5:26
[a]Phil 2:3

Koine Greek

Gal. 5:1 Τη ελευθερια ουν η χριστος ημας ηλευθερωσεν, στηκετε, και μη παλιν ζυγω δουλειας ενεχεσθε.

Gal. 5:2 Ιδε, εγω Παυλος λεγω υμιν, οτι εαν περιτεμνησθε, χριστος υμας ουδεν ωφελησει. ³ Μαρτυρομαι δε παλιν παντι ανθρωπω περιτεμνομενω, οτι οφειλετης εστιν ολον τον νομον ποιησαι. ⁴ Κατηργηθητε απο του χριστου, οιτινες εν νομω δικαιουσθε· της χαριτος ˊ εξεπεσατε. ˋ ⁵ Ημεις γαρ πνευματι εκ πιστεως ελπιδα δικαιοσυνης απεκδεχομεθα. ⁶ Εν γαρ χριστω Ιησου ουτε περιτομη τι ισχυει, ουτε ακροβυστια, αλλα πιστις δι’ αγαπης ενεργουμενη. ⁷ Ετρεχετε καλως· τις υμας ενεκοψεν τη αληθεια μη πειθεσθαι; ⁸ Η πεισμονη ουκ εκ του καλουντος υμας. ⁹ Μικρα ζυμη ολον το φυραμα ζυμοι. ¹⁰ Εγω πεποιθα εις υμας εν κυριω, οτι ουδεν αλλο φρονησετε· ο δε ταρασσων υμας βαστασει το κριμα, οστις αν η. ¹¹ Εγω δε, αδελφοι, ει περιτομην ετι κηρυσσω, τι ετι διωκομαι; Αρα κατηργηται το σκανδαλον του σταυρου. ¹² Οφελον και αποκοφονται οι αναστατουντες υμας.

Gal. 5:13 Υμεις γαρ επ’ ελευθερια εκληθητε, αδελφοι· μονον μη την ελευθεριαν εις αφορμην τη σαρκι, αλλα δια της αγαπης δουλευετε αλληλοις. ¹⁴ Ο γαρ πας νομος εν ενι λογω πληρουται, εν τω, Αγαπησεις τον πλησιον σου ως εαυτον. ¹⁵ Ει δε αλληλους δακνετε και κατεσθιετε, βλεπετε μη υπο αλληλων αναλωθητε.

Gal. 5:16 Λεγω δε, πνευματι περιπατειτε, και επιθυμιαν σαρκος ου μη τελεσητε. ¹⁷ Η γαρ σαρξ επιθυμει κατα του πνευματος, το δε πνευμα κατα της σαρκος· ταυτα δε αντικειται αλληλοις, ινα μη α αν θελητε, ταυτα ποιητε. ¹⁸ Ει δε πνευματι αγεσθε, ουκ εστε υπο νομον. ¹⁹ Φανερα δε εστιν τα εργα της σαρκος, ατινα εστιν μοιχεια, πορνεια, ακαθαρσια, ασελγεια, ²⁰ ειδωλολατρεια, φαρμακεια, εχθραι, ερεις, ζηλοι, θυμοι, εριθειαι, διχοστασιαι, αιρεσεις, ²¹ φθονοι, φονοι, μεθαι, κωμοι, και τα ομοια τουτοις· α προλεγω υμιν, καθως και προειπον, οτι οι τα τοιαυτα πρασσοντες βασιλειαν θεου ου κληρονομησουσιν. ²² Ο δε καρπος του πνευματος εστιν αγαπη, χαρα, ειρηνη, μακροθυμια, χρηστοτης, αγαθωσυνη, πιστις, ²³ πραοτης, εγκρατεια· κατα των τοιουτων ουκ εστιν νομος. ²⁴ Οι δε του χριστου, την σαρκα εσταυρωσαν συν τοις παθημασιν και ταις επιθυμιαις.

Gal. 5:25 Ει ζωμεν πνευματι, πνευματι και στοιχωμεν. ²⁶ Μη γινωμεθα κενοδοξοι, αλληλους προκαλουμενοι, αλληλοις φθονουντες.

Language

Process of Discovery

Linguistics Section

Linguistic Structure

[Transition] Gal. 5:1   [1a]It was for freedom that Christ set us free; therefore [b]keep standing firm and do not be subject again to a [c]yoke of slavery.

A Gal. 5:2   Behold I, [a]Paul, say to you that if you receive [b]circumcision, Christ will be of no benefit to you. **3** And I [a]testify again to every man who receives [b]circumcision, that he is under obligation to [c]keep the whole Law. **4** You have been severed from Christ, you who [1]are seeking to be justified by law; you have [a]fallen from grace. **5** For we [1]through the Spirit, [2]by faith, are [a]waiting for the hope of righteousness. **6** For in [a]Christ Jesus [b]neither circumcision nor uncircumcision means anything, but [c]faith working through love.

> **B Gal. 5:7**   You were [a]running well; who hindered you from obeying the truth? **8** This persuasion *did* not *come* from [a]Him who calls you. **9** [a]A little leaven leavens the whole lump *of dough*. **10** [a]I have confidence [1]in you in the Lord that you [b]will adopt no other view; but the one who is [c]disturbing you will bear his judgment, whoever he is.

> **B' 11** But I, brethren, if I still preach circumcision, why am I still [a]persecuted? Then [b]the stumbling block of the cross has been abolished. **12** I wish that [a]those who are troubling you would even [1b]mutilate themselves.

A' Gal. 5:13   For you were called to [a]freedom, brethren; [b]only *do* not *turn* your freedom into an opportunity for the flesh, but through love [c]serve one another. **14** For [a]the whole Law is fulfilled in one word, in the *statement,* "[b]YOU SHALL LOVE YOUR NEIGHBOR AS YOURSELF."

A 15 But if you [a]bite and devour one another, take care that you are not consumed by one another.

> **B Gal. 5:16**   But I say, [a]walk by the Spirit, and you will not carry out [b]the desire of the flesh. **17** For [a]the flesh [1]sets its desire against the Spirit, and the Spirit against the flesh; for these are in opposition to one another, [b]so that you may not do the

things that you [2]please. **[18]** But if you are [d]led by the Spirit, [b]you are not under the Law.

C [19] Now the deeds of the flesh are evident, which are: [1a]immorality, impurity, sensuality, **[20]** idolatry, [a]sorcery, enmities, [b]strife, jealousy, outbursts of anger, [c]disputes, dissensions, [1d]factions, **[21]** envying, [a]drunkenness, carousing, and things like these, of which I forewarn you, just as I have forewarned you, that those who practice such things will not [b]inherit the kingdom of God.

C' [22] But [a]the fruit of the Spirit is [b]love, joy, peace, patience, kindness, goodness, faithfulness, **[23]** gentleness, [a]self-control; against such things [b]there is no law.

B' [24] Now those who [1]belong to [a]Christ Jesus have [b]crucified the flesh with its passions and [c]desires. **Gal. 5:25** If we live by the Spirit, let us also [1]walk [a]by the Spirit.

A [26] Let us not become [a]boastful, challenging one another, envying one another.

Discussion

This chapter has two chiasms. Each chiasm has two main points.

Questioning the Passage

1. What does Paul think the Spirit is?

"Paul uses 'spirit' to indicate the inner nature of a person."[25]

2. What is the yoke of slavery? (v. 1)

The yoke of slavery is the rules and regulations that govern how people live.

---

[25] Revandybooks, "St Paul and the Spirit. It Was Central to Paul's Faith," Bible in brief, November 6, 2018, https://www.bibleinbrief.org/2018/11/06/paul-and-the-spirit/.

3. What does "we through the Spirit by faith" mean? (v. 5)

    Considering the spirit is a reference to the inner nature of a person, then this statement means that it is the faith that Paul and his colleagues have in the meaning of Yeshua's life and death which controls their belief that they will find righteousness. Paul and his colleagues believed that Yeshua's life and death was the only requirement for righteousness. Martin Luther believed it was through a faith in Yeshua that righteousness came, thus discounting the Catholic belief of works righteousness.

4. What does "waiting for the hope of righteousness" mean? (v. 6)

    The hope of righteousness is the hope that on judgment day, Yeshua will stand next to a person and Yeshua's righteousness will be imputed. Therefore, on judgment day, the LORD will see Yeshua's righteousness as the person's righteousness.

5. What do verses one to six mean?

    Paul did not believe that anyone who wanted to follow Yeshua had to become Jewish, nor follow any of the Jewish laws. Paul places a caveat on demonstrating a faith in Yeshua by saying, "faith working through love." To follow, Yeshua means to love one's neighbors.

6. What does verse nine means?

    Paul was concerned that other expressions of Christianity were coming to the congregation and telling them that Paul's way was not Yeshua's way. Paul uses the metaphor of yeast (leaven) in the same way that Yeshua used it in the

Gospels. The outsider ideas, if allowed into the community, would spread and infect the entire group. Paul warned the congregation not to allow that to happen.

7. What is the judgment? (v. 10)

The judgment referred to is the punishment that an outsider will receive for spreading different views of Yeshua's life that contradict Paul.

8. What is the offense of the cross? (v. 11)

The offense of the cross is found in the Peshitta. The NASB says "the stumbling block." For the Jewish people, the cross was the worst way to die. The Romans kept the body on the cross after death. A few days later, the body fell off the cross. Birds and dogs would then eat the rotting flesh. This desecration of the body was considered an unacceptable way to die. In Paul's day, how can the cross be considered a way to Heaven? This is the problem with the cross as a symbol to represent Yeshua. Over time, it became the sign of the Proto-Orthodox church. In the first century CE, it was the fish that symbolized the believers in Yeshua. Paul probably had difficulty explaining to Jews why the cross is salvation. For the Gentile Mithras converts, they would not have seen any problem with the cross as a means of salvation. Mithras died for the sins of his followers. When Paul substituted Yeshua for Mithras, Yeshua became the one who died for the sins of his followers.

9. What is the call to freedom? (v. 13)

Paul believed that if a Jew became a Yeshua follower, that the person did not have to follow the Torah Laws. Paul believed that the Torah laws were a hinderance and did not lead to salvation. There are too many Laws (613) that it is not possible to execute everyone successfully. Paul was trained to follow the

Law. Paul abandoned these teachings. Paul did not have it easy trying to convince Jews to turn to Yeshua as the Messiah. The book of Acts says that he eventually turned away from Judaism and worked on converting Gentiles. The Mithras House churches were the obvious answer to Paul's quest. Why Paul turned from a persecutor of the Yeshua movement to become its biggest evangelist is not known.

10. Why is the whole law not including love God? (v. 14)

Paul did not include loving God because he assumed everyone would want to love God. It is surprising that he mentions a component of the Law that he is arguing against.

11. Why is Paul denouncing the Law but then says that they need to follow one of the two summaries of the Law? (v. 14)

As mentioned earlier, it is a surprise to find this statement about loving neighbor. The Sage Hillel said that a person could learn the Torah Law while standing on one foot. The Law is to love God and love neighbor. Everything else is commentary. The general thought is even though Paul tells the congregation that they do not have to follow the Jewish Law, the idea of loving neighbor is important because it leads to an ethical life. The members of the congregation needed to behave to please Yeshua. Loving neighbor is definitely a way to do this since Yeshua said it was one of the two great commandments. Gentiles reading this letter might not know that this is a one-half summary of the Jewish Law.

12. What does "walk by the Spirit" mean? (v. 16)

   To "walk by the Spirit" means to behave in a manner that one knows is ethical and moral. Paul uses this type of phrase often in his letters. For Paul, every person knows it is important to live an ethical life. There are plenty of people who do not follow this belief, however overall, it is important to maintain the ethics that Yeshua expressed during his life. It is interesting to note that since Paul did not learn directly from Yeshua, it becomes a question of where he got these ideas. He adopted his views to satisfy Gentiles. There are a few things that he insisted from Jewish tradition, which are described in this chapter.

13. When did forgiveness enter the church? (v. 21)

   Verse twenty-one begs the question of when forgiveness for sin entered the Proto-Orthodox church? History says that the early church did not tolerate the committing of sin after one was baptized into the faith. One died with Christ and was raised as a new life with Christ. Therefore, sin was washed away and was not to be committed again. The idea of excommunication was not something Yeshua proposed. Rather, it was the leaders' way of controlling people. Clearly, the new members to the community were told how to live. Violations to these "laws" would cause excommunication. It is not historically known when forgiveness of sins committed after baptism entered the church. There are church denominations which still hold on to excommunication or refusal of accepting a person as a member if they committed a sin. For example, some sects of the Brethren church will not allow a person to become a church member if they were ever divorced. Where is the forgiveness for that mistake? In that church, it is an unforgivable sin which requires the person to be outside the body of Christ. To maintain power, the church employed excommunication for those who committed sin after baptism, even though Yeshua is believed to have died for the forgiveness of sin (like Mithras did).

14. Why is forgiveness not a fruit of the Spirit? (v. 22)

Teshuva (repentance and forgiveness) is not listed as a fruit of the Spirit because it is a basic force in the Universe. The Spirit of the Torah objected to the LORD about the creation of humanity because of sin. The LORD assured the Torah that forgiveness would be a basic building block of the universe and would exist everywhere. The idea of repentance is key to the universe. It is unfortunate that there are people today who do not practice forgiveness. Yeshua said that one must be able to forgive in order to be forgiven.

15. Where did Paul get the list of the fruits of the Spirit? (v. 22)

This is a list that Paul developed.

16. What does "crucified the flesh" mean? (v. 24)

"The concept of crucifying the flesh comes from the apostle Paul's words in Galatians 5:24: "Those who belong to Christ Jesus have crucified the flesh with its passions and desires." In this verse, it's clear that crucifying the flesh is not something done *to* the believer, but *by* the believer: "Those who belong to Christ have crucified the flesh."

The "flesh" that must be crucified is the sin principle that exists in our fallen human nature. In this world we live in fleshly bodies, and the body, being weak (Mark 14:38), is the gateway to sin. Our bodies, though not sinful in themselves, naturally crave comfort and pleasure, and they too often succumb to temptation, producing the works of the flesh (Galatians 5:19–21). Sin entrenches itself in the flesh, which becomes dominated by iniquity of all kinds. It is the sinful passions and wayward deeds of the flesh that Christians must crucify.

In other places, Paul speaks of a crucifixion that happens *to* the believer through his or her union with Jesus Christ: "I have been crucified with Christ and I no longer live, but Christ lives in me" (Galatians 2:20; see also Romans 6:6). But in Galatians 5:24, it is the believer who has taken action. *Crucify the flesh* describes a deliberate putting to death of the old sin nature."[26]

17. What does "walk by the Spirit" mean? (v. 25)

"Ways You Can Walk in the Spirit

So, Paul called believers to walk away from the old ideas about salvation that were embedded in rabbinical Judaism of the first century as well as in Gentile pagan religions. Believers must walk a new way: in the Spirit. But what does that mean?

Jesus said, "So I say to you, ask, and it will be given to you; seek, and you will find; knock, and it will be opened to you" (Luke 11:9). J.J. Packer in his classic work on the subject, *Keep in Step with the Spirit,* reminds us that the beginning of a walk with God through the power and presence of the Holy Spirit begins with God's first step to us in prayer. Packer tells us that of those who ask for God's Spirit "Many have been staggered at the wealth of God's answer in experience to this request."

To walk in the Spirit is to:

---

[26] GotQuestions.org, "Home," GotQuestions.org, December 18, 2019, https://www.gotquestions.org/crucify-the-flesh.html.

1. Walk away from sin. Sin is disobedience to the revealed will of God. Walk away from sin by having the sin nature cleansed by pure righteous life of Jesus. When you receive Him, He gets your sins and you get His life. Walk, therefore, to the cross and leave your sins with Christ Jesus, by faith, today.

2. Walk away from any other supposed "way" to God. The context in Galatia can be ours, too. Walk away from any idea that you can please God or satisfy God's righteous requirements and His punishment for sin by doing something yourself. You can't. It is cosmically impossible. But what God has required, God has provided through His Son, Jesus our Lord. Walk away from the bad idea of salvation by works, by ritual, or by any action or idea or person other than the Lord Jesus.

3. Walk towards the truth of God's Word. To walk in the Spirit is to walk in the Word. God the Holy Spirit breathed out the very Word of God. The Bible says that this, then, became flesh in the person of Jesus our Lord. Walk in His Word today and every day. Walk in His Word through this website and others like it that seek to keep you grounded in God's Word. Seek His Word and you will find Him. He will fill you as you breath in that sacred Word that He breathed out.

4. Walk towards the light of the love of Jesus. Jesus said that He is the light of the world. To walk in the Spirit is to be following Jesus, for the Spirit speaks of Christ Jesus. The Spirit magnifies the name of Jesus. And the light of Christ is His all-pervasive grace and love.

5. Walk in prayer and total dependence upon the Lord. Seek Christ and His life in daily prayer, in public prayer, and in meditation on God's Word. You, too,

will be "staggered" by God's response to those who seek Him with all of their heart, soul, and mind.

To do these things is to walk in the Holy Spirit. The Bible says that Enoch walked with God. One day Enoch kept walking. He walked right into heave (<u>Genesis 5:21-24</u>).

To walk in the Spirit will be to spend and be spent in the glorious life of following the Lord Jesus Christ. This walk will ultimately pass through either the portal of death or the Second Coming. And you will step, in the Spirit, into the very presence of God.[27]

18. Why are the character traits in verse twenty-six not a part of nineteen through twenty-one?

Perhaps Paul forgot to include these character traits when he wrote verses nineteen through twenty-one. Paper was expensive, so one did not destroy the letter and reset it over an omission. A second idea is that he wanted to more strongly express these traits.

Phrase Study

1. αποκοπτω fut. αποκοψω; (v. 12)

   a. of body parts

   b. of noncorporal things τα σχοινια *cut the ropes*

---

[27] "'Walk in the Spirit' - Galatians 5:16 Meaning and Application Today," biblestudytools.com, September 23, 2020, https://www.biblestudytools.com/bible-study/topical-studies/what-does-it-mean-to-walk-in-the-spirit.html.

The translation of "NOT MUTILATE" is not proper. Paul is referring to people arriving in Galatia trying to change the congregation and Paul wanted them excommunicated from the church. This verse could be used to justified denominations because if a person disagrees with the church's doctrine they are to be removed, according to Paul. So, it is not Yeshua's church but Paul's church since he said exclude people who did not think like him. An option is to convert those who are saying something different. Perhaps he said live together with people of different ideas but do not let their ideas change you. Is Paul preaching a unity of different ideas about Yeshua? The answer is no. For Paul, he believed he had the only explanation of Yeshua's work. Unfortunately, Yeshua's doctrine about what he was preaching was not written. Paul shows churches how to be territorial. This can be seen today while the mainline churches separate over the cultural change in 2020 and beyond. The United Methodist Church told churches that do not agree with Progressive Christianity and an absence of the Bible to leave the denomination. Unfortunately, the UMC demands huge cash payments from churches to leave. The history of the Christian church is that when people developed a different doctrine than the accepted church doctrine, they were forced to leave. The Reformation is a prime example of this idea. Martin Luther's followers did not agree with some doctrines of the Catholic church. These people were forced to leave the church. After the Reformation, denominations grew to over 1,000 today.

Thoughts

Paul's ego is on full display in this chapter. He believed that he had the only understanding of what Yeshua's life was about. The Proto-Orthodox resulted from Paul's conversion of the Mithras House churches. Thus, at the turn of the first century CE the bishops wanted to find all the Pauline letters they could, and they made them sacred. By making the letters sacred and including them in the Scriptures the early bishops elevated Paul to an almost Messiah level. Since the church searched for documents which justified the theology and doctrine, they developed, it made sense to find Paul's letters. After all, the letters and Mithras rituals are the basis of Christian doctrine today.

It is interesting that Paul told the Galatians to reject anyone that thought differently than the way he taught them. Paul defined his expression of Christianity and told his church to destroy all other expressions. Throughout the early history of the church, that is exactly what happened. The first split of the church in 1096 CE between the Catholic and Orthodox church could be seen in this chapter. The two sides could not come to an agreement over Trinity. Therefore, they split apart. Today each side still says that the other side is heretics. The Reformation was another split inside the Catholic church. Since 1517, the idea of church splintering has become part of the church's DNA.

Chapter Six

Language

Peshitta	New American Standard 1995
Gal. 6:1 My brethren, if one of you should be overtaken in a fault, do ye who are of the Spirit recover him, in a spirit of meekness: and be ye cautious, lest ye also be tempted. **2** And bear ye one another's burdens, that so ye may fulfill the law of the Messiah. **3** For if any one thinketh himself to be something, when he is not, he deceiveth himself. **4** But let a man examine his own conduct; and then his glorying will be within himself, and not in others. **5** For every man must take up his own load. **6** And let him that heareth the word, communicate to him who instructeth him, in all good things. **7** Do not mistake; God is not deceived; for what a man soweth, that also will he reap. **8** He who soweth in the flesh, reapeth from the flesh corruption: and he who soweth in the Spirit, will from the Spirit reap life everlasting. **9** And while we do what is good, let it not be wearisome to us; for the time will come when we shall reap, and it will not be tedious to us. **10** Now, therefore, while we have the opportunity, let us practice good works towards all men, and especially towards them of the household of faith. **11** Behold, this epistle have I written to you with my own hand. **12** They who are	**Gal. 6:1** [a]Brethren, even if [1]anyone is caught in any trespass, you who are [b]spiritual, [c]restore such a one [d]in a spirit of gentleness; *each one* looking to yourself, so that you too will not be tempted. **2** [a]Bear one another's burdens, and thereby fulfill [b]the law of Christ. **3** For [a]if anyone thinks he is something when he is nothing, he deceives himself. **4** But each one must [a]examine his own work, and then he will have *reason for* [b]boasting in regard to himself alone, and not in regard to another. **5** For [a]each one will bear his own load. **Gal. 6:6** [a]The one who is taught [b]the word is to share all good things with the one who teaches *him*. **7** [a]Do not be deceived, [b]God is not mocked; for [c]whatever a man sows, this he will also reap. **8** [a]For the one who sows to his own flesh will from the flesh reap [b]corruption, but [c]the one who sows to the Spirit will from the Spirit reap eternal life. **9** [a]Let us not lose heart in doing good, for in due time we will reap if we [b]do not grow weary. **10** So then, [1a]while we have opportunity, let us do good to all people, and especially to those who are of the [b]household of [c]the faith. **Gal. 6:11** See with what large letters I [1]am writing to you [a]with my own hand. **12** Those who desire [a]to make a good

disposed to glory in the flesh, they urge you to become circumcised, only that they may not be persecuted on account of the cross of the Messiah. **13** For not even they themselves, who are circumcised, keep the law: but they wish you to become circumcised, that they may glory in your flesh. **14** But as for me, let me not glory, except in the cross of our Lord Jesus the Messiah; by whom the world is crucified to me, and I am crucified to the world. **15** For circumcision is nothing; neither is uncircumcision; but a new creation. **16** And they who press forward in this path, peace be on them, and mercy; and on the Israel of God. **17** Henceforth let no one put trouble upon me; for I bear in my body the marks of our Lord Jesus the Messiah. **18** My brethren, the grace of our Lord Jesus the Messiah, be with your spirit. Amen.

showing in the flesh try to [b]compel you to be circumcised, simply so that they [c]will not be persecuted [1]for the cross of Christ. **13** For those who [1]are circumcised do not even [a]keep [2]the Law themselves, but they desire to have you circumcised so that they may [b]boast in your flesh. **14** But [a]may it never be that I would boast, [b]except in the cross of our Lord Jesus Christ, [c]through [1]which the world has been crucified to me, and [d]I to the world. **15** For [a]neither is circumcision anything, nor uncircumcision, but a [b]new [1]creation. **16** And those who will [1]walk by this rule, peace and mercy *be* upon them, and upon the [a]Israel of God.

Gal. 6:17 From now on let no one cause trouble for me, for I bear on my body the [a]brand-marks of Jesus.

Gal. 6:18 [a]The grace of our Lord Jesus Christ be [b]with your spirit, [c]brethren. Amen.

References to the New American Standard 1995

Galatians 6:1
[1]Gr *anthropos*
[a]Gal 6:18; 1 Thess 4:1
[b]1 Cor 2:15
[c]2 Cor 2:7; 2 Thess 3:15; Heb 12:13; James 5:19f
[d]1 Cor 4:21

Galatians 6:2
[a]Rom 15:1
[b]Rom 8:2; 1 Cor 9:21; James 1:25; 2:12; 2 Pet 3:2

Galatians 6:3
[a]Acts 5:36; 1 Cor 3:18; 2 Cor 12:11

Galatians 6:4
[a]1 Cor 11:28
[b]Phil 1:26

Galatians 6:5
[a]Prov 9:12; Rom 14:12; 1 Cor 3:8

Galatians 6:6
[a]1 Cor 9:11, 14
[b]2 Tim 4:2

Galatians 6:7
[a]1 Cor 6:9
[b]Job 13:9
[c]2 Cor 9:6

Galatians 6:8
[a]Job 4:8; Hos 8:7; Rom 6:21
[b]1 Cor 15:42
[c]Rom 8:11; James 3:18

Galatians 6:9

[a]1 Cor 15:58; 2 Cor 4:1
[b]Matt 10:22; Heb 12:3, 5; James 5:7f

Galatians 6:10
[1]Or *as*
[a]Prov 3:27; John 12:35
[b]Eph 2:19; Heb 3:6; 1 Pet 2:5; 4:17
[c]Acts 6:7; Gal 1:23

Galatians 6:11
[1]Or *have written*
[a]1 Cor 16:21

Galatians 6:12
[1]Or *because of*
[a]Matt 23:27f
[b]Acts 15:1
[c]Gal 5:11

Galatians 6:13
[1]Two early mss read *have been*
[2]Or *law*
[a]Rom 2:25
[b]Phil 3:3

Galatians 6:14
[1]Or *whom*
[a]Luke 20:16; Gal 2:17; 3:21
[b]1 Cor 2:2
[c]Gal 2:20; Col 2:20
[d]Rom 6:2, 6; Gal 2:19f; 5:24

Galatians 6:15
[1]Or *creature*
[a]Rom 2:26, 28; 1 Cor 7:19; Gal 5:6
[b]2 Cor 5:17; Eph 2:10, 15; 4:24; Col 3:10

Galatians 6:16
[1]Or *follow this rule*
[a]Rom 9:6; Gal 3:7, 29; Phil 3:3

Galatians 6:17
[a]Is 44:5; Ezek 9:4; 2 Cor 4:10; 11:23; Rev 13:16

Galatians 6:18
[a]Rom 16:20
[b]2 Tim 4:22
[c]Acts 1:15; Rom 1:13; Gal 3:15; 4:12, 28, 31

Koine Greek

Gal. 6:1   Αδελφοι, εαν και προληφθη ανθρωπος εν τινι παραπτωματι, υμεις οι πνευματικοι καταρτιζετε τον τοιουτον εν πνευματι πραοτητος, σκοπων σεαυτον μη και συ πειρασθης. [2] Αλληλων τα βαρη βασταζετε, και ουτως αναπληρωσατε τον νομον του χριστου. [3] Ει γαρ δοκει τις ειναι τι, μηδεν ων, εαυτον φρεναπατα· [4] το δε εργον εαυτου δοκιμαζετω εκαστος, και τοτε εις εαυτον μονον το καυχημα εξει, και ουκ εις τον ετερον. [5] Εκαστος γαρ το ιδιον φορτιον βαστασει.

Gal. 6:6   Κοινωνειτω δε ο κατηχουμενος τον λογον τω κατηχουντι εν πασιν αγαθοις. [7] Μη πλανασθε, θεος ου μυκτηριζεται· ο γαρ εαν σπειρη ανθρωπος, τουτο και θερισει. [8] Οτι ο σπειρων εις την σαρκα εαυτου, εκ της σαρκος θερισει φθοραν· ο δε σπειρων εις το πνευμα, εκ του πνευματος θερισει ζωην αιωνιον. [9] Το δε καλον ποιουντες μη εκκακωμεν· καιρω γαρ ιδιω θερισομεν, μη εκλυομενοι. [10] Αρα ουν ως καιρον εχομεν, εργαζωμεθα το αγαθον προς παντας, μαλιστα δε προς τους οικειους της πιστεως.

Gal. 6:11   Ιδετε πηλικοις υμιν γραμμασιν εγραψα τη εμη χειρι. [12] Οσοι θελουσιν ευπροσωπησαι εν σαρκι, ουτοι αναγκαζουσιν υμας περιτεμνεσθαι, μονον ινα μη τω σταυρω του χριστου διωκωνται. [13] Ουδε γαρ οι περιτετμημενοι αυτοι νομον φυλασσουσιν· αλλα θελουσιν υμας περιτεμνεσθαι, ινα εν τη υμετερα σαρκι καυχησωνται. [14] Εμοι δε μη γενοιτο καυχασθαι ει μη εν τω σταυρω του κυριου ημων Ιησου χριστου· δι’ ου εμοι κοσμος εσταυρωται, καγω τω κοσμω. [15] Εν γαρ χριστω Ιησου ουτε περιτομη τι ισχυει, ουτε ακροβυστια, αλλα καινη κτισις. [16] Και οσοι τω κανονι τουτω στοιχησουσιν, ειρηνη επ’ αυτους, και ελεος, και επι τον Ισραηλ του θεου.

Gal. 6:17   Του λοιπου, κοπους μοι μηδεις παρεχετω· εγω γαρ τα στιγματα του κυριου Ιησου εν τω σωματι μου βασταζω.

Gal. 6:18   Η χαρις του κυριου ημων Ιησου χριστου μετα του πνευματος υμων, αδελφοι. Αμην.

Language

Process of Discovery

Linguistics Section

Linguistic Structure

[Help one another] Gal. 6:1 *a*Brethren, even if [1]anyone is caught in any trespass, you who are *b*spiritual, *c*restore such a one *d*in a spirit of gentleness; *each one* looking to yourself, so that you too will not be tempted. **2** *a*Bear one another's burdens, and thereby fulfill *b*the law of Christ. **3** For *a*if anyone thinks he is something when he is nothing, he deceives himself. **4** But each one must *a*examine his own work, and then he will have *reason for* *b*boasting in regard to himself alone, and not in regard to another. **5** For *a*each one will bear his own load.

[Exhortations] Gal. 6:6 *a*The one who is taught *b*the word is to share all good things with the one who teaches *him*. **7** *a*Do not be deceived, *b*God is not mocked; for *c*whatever a man sows, this he will also reap. **8** *a*For the one who sows to his own flesh will from the flesh reap *b*corruption, but *c*the one who sows to the Spirit will from the Spirit reap eternal life. **9** *a*Let us not lose heart in doing good, for in due time we will reap if we *b*do not grow weary. **10** So then, [1]*a*while we have opportunity, let us do good to all people, and especially to those who are of the *b*household of *c*the faith.

[Well thought out letter] Gal. 6:11 See with what large letters I [1]am writing to you *a*with my own hand. **12** Those who desire *a*to make a good showing in the flesh try to *b*compel you to be circumcised, simply so that they *c*will not be persecuted [1]for the cross of Christ. **13** For those who [1]are circumcised do not even *a*keep [2]the Law themselves, but they desire to have you circumcised so that they may *b*boast in your flesh. **14** But *a*may it never be that I would boast, *b*except in the cross of our Lord Jesus Christ, *c*through [1]which the world has been crucified to me, and *d*I to the world. **15** For *a*neither is circumcision anything, nor uncircumcision, but a *b*new [1]creation. **16** And those who will [1]walk by this rule, peace and mercy *be* upon them, and upon the *a*Israel of God.

[Benediction] Gal. 6:17 From now on let no one cause trouble for me, for I bear on my body the *a*brand-marks of Jesus. **Gal. 6:18** *a*The grace of our Lord Jesus Christ be *b*with your spirit, *c*brethren. Amen.

Discussion

Paul concludes his letter with the exhortation to the community to love and care for each other. From the points of the letter, this community was not formed in the manner that the communities in Acts were formed. The idea of having to turn over all property to the apostles is not a part of Paul's work.

Questioning the Passage

1. What does it mean to be spiritual? (v. 1)

   "Paul has repeatedly spoken elsewhere in Galatians of all Christians as being possessed by and in possession of God's Spirit (cf. 3:2–5, 14; 4:6, 29; 5:5, 16–18, 22–23, 25; 6:8). There is, therefore, no reason to doubt and abundant reason to believe that Paul here uses this designation with approval in speaking about *all* his converts in Galatia. They are, despite their legal and libertine enticements, "the true spirituals" simply because by being "in Christ" they have become the recipients of God's Spirit. So by reminding his converts of their status as πνευματικοί Paul calls on them to live up to that status".[28]

2. What is a spirit of gentleness? (v. 1)

   This is one fruit of the spirit from chapter five verse twenty-two.

3. What is the law of Christ? (v. 2)

   "To understand what Paul meant by "the law of Christ" here, much depends on how we understand the purpose and focus of 5:13–6:10. For if we view 5:13–6:10 as a continuation of Paul's arguments and exhortations against the

---

[28] Longenecker, R. N. (1990). *Galatians* (Vol. 41, p. 273). Word, Incorporated.

Judaizing threat, then "the law of Christ" must have relevance to what the Judaizers were proposing. One can then, in fact, wonder why this expression does not appear earlier in the Galatian letter. Likewise, if we take 5:13–6:10 to reflect the polemics of Paul's antinomistic stance, then νόμος here may very well be used in contradistinction to the Judaizers' usage. If, however, 5:13–6:10 be seen more in terms of the libertine issues that were also present in the churches of Galatia, then "the law of Christ" may be taken as an expression stemming from Paul's own ethical vocabulary that is used here"[29]

4. What does it mean to bear one another's burdens? (v. 2)

    Paul said that each member of the congregation should help each other without pretense. Members of the congregation were to help another person if possible. One should help another person because they want to do it.

5. What does it mean to be nothing? (v. 3)

    "Understanding, then, the statement of v 3 to be a traditional maxim of the Greco-Roman world, Paul uses it by way of general support for his directive to "bear one another's oppressive burdens" of v 2. His point, it seems, is that conceit—that is, thinking oneself to be something when in actuality we are nothing (as the maxim has it)—results in making one unwilling to bear others' burdens. In effect, the maxim quoted here roughly parallels the exhortation of 5:26, with the warnings against conceit of 5:26 and 6:3 serving as something of an *inclusio* for the exhortations regarding restoring the wayward and bearing one another's oppressive burdens of 6:1–2."[30]

---

[29] IBID.

[30] IBID.

6. What do verses five and six mean?

Paul encouraged the congregation to carry their own burdens. He was concerned that some of the people were oppressing the poor members. To be a follower of Yeshua meant not only not to oppress the poor but also to help the poor. Paul could also be referring to the mental burdens, worries and cares of the that time.[31] Paul wanted all members of the congregation to be treated equally.

7. What does verse eight mean?

This is an allegorical statement. When one works to benefit one's flesh it can turn into a corrupt soul. When one works to benefit the soul it is equivalent to Yeshua saying that one must store treasures in Heaven. These types of actions bolster the soul when it enters Heaven.

8. What does large letters mean? (v. 11)

"Hellenistic letters in Paul's day usually exhibited two styles of handwriting: a more practiced, carefully constructed script of an amanuensis or secretary in most of the letter and the cruder or more casual style of the sender in the subscription (see *Introduction*, pp. lviii–lx). Paul, in fact, seems to have followed the practice of using an amanuensis for the writing of all his letters, though his amanuenses were personal companions or able fellow believers of the various churches rather than professional scribes (see *Introduction*, pp. lx–lxi). And here by the phrase τῇ ἐμῇ χειρί, "in my own hand," Paul's recipients are alerted to the fact that they are not now reading and/or hearing what an amanuensis has

---

[31] Rocco A. Errico and George M. Lamsa, *Aramaic Light on Galatians through Hebrews: A Commentary Based on Aramaic, the Language of Jesus, and Ancient near Eastern Customs* (Smyma, GA: Noohra Foundation, 2005).

written down on his behalf but Paul's own statements that he has inscribed himself."[32]

9. What does verse twelve mean?

Paul was again showing his deep concern that Jews who were learning about Christ from Peter will come to the congregation and urge them to be circumcised for Yeshua. For Paul, the main thing a person had to do was to have faith in the events of Good Friday through Easter morning. Yeshua was crucified and rose again three days later.

10. What does "persecuted for the Cross of Christ" mean? (v. 12)

This is oppression of being a believer in Yeshua on the cross. Eventually, it was the Roman government that persecuted the Proto-Orthodox church. For Paul, the persecutor was the Jewish Temple in Jerusalem. Those leaders did not view Yeshua as the Messiah but as a troublemaker. Paul said to the Galatians that they should never give up their belief in the cross of Yeshua.

11. What does verse fourteen mean?

Paul uses the cross as a symbol. "The world is crucified unto me" is an expression that means that it destroyed forever all the evils of the world and its erroneous philosophies and teachings when Yeshua died on the cross. Yeshua arose from death in a spiritual body to become the first fruits of a new order based on meekness and loving kindness.[33]

---

[32] Longenecker, R. N. (1990). *Galatians* (Vol. 41, p. 289). Word, Incorporated.

[33] Rocco A. Errico and George M. Lamsa, *Aramaic Light on Galatians through Hebrews: A Commentary Based on Aramaic, the Language of Jesus, and Ancient near Eastern Customs* (Smyma, GA: Noohra Foundation, 2005).

12. What does verse sixteen mean?

"But while the first part of v 16 may seem rather straightforward, not at all clear are (1) the form and extent of the peace benediction that appears in the midst of the verse (assuming the usual punctuation) and (2) how the last clause of the verse relates to what precedes it (assuming that this last clause is something of an appendage). The issues here boil down to two: Does Paul have in mind one group of people on whom he pronounces an expanded peace benediction ("peace and mercy") or is he visualizing two groups of people, the first being the objects of his peace benediction and the second the objects of his mercy benediction? And what does Paul mean by the expression "the Israel of God," for the term "Israel" is never applied elsewhere in the NT to Gentile Christians but always to Jews?

Traditionally it has been assumed that Paul's calling Gentile Christians "the Israel of God" means that the Christian church has taken the place of the Jewish nation as "the true, spiritual Israel" (cf. Justin, *Dial.* 11.5; see also, e.g., John Chrysostom, *Commentary on the Epistle to the Galatians,* ad loc.; N. A. Dahl, *Judaica* 6 [1950] 161–70). But as W. D. Davies aptly notes: "If this proposal were correct one would have expected to find support for it in Rom. ix–xi where Paul extensively deals with 'Israel' " (*NTS* 24 [1977] 1 0–11 n. 2).

It is sometimes argued that the phrase "the Israel of God" is Paul's way of referring to nonjudaizing Jewish Christians of Galatia (cf., e.g., G. Schrenk, *Judaica* 5 [1949] 81–94; idem, *Judaica* 6 [1950] 170–90; D. W. B. Robinson, *ABR* 13 [1965] 2 9–44). Others see here an eschatological reference comparable to πᾶς Ἰσραήλ ("all Israel") of Rom 11:26–27, with that expression understood as the totality of Jews who will be saved when "the deliverer will come from Zion" (cf., e.g., Mussner, *Galaterbrief*, 417; Bruce, *Galatians*, 275). Yet all of the views that take "the Israel of God" to refer to Jews and not Gentiles, while supportable by reference to Paul's wider usage (or nonusage) of terms and expressions, fail to take seriously enough the context of the Galatian letter itself. For in a letter where Paul is concerned to treat as indifferent the distinctions that separate Jewish and Gentile Christians and to argue for the equality of Gentile believers with Jewish believers, it is difficult to see him at the very end of that letter pronouncing a benediction (or benedictions) that would serve to separate groups within his churches—whether he means by "the Israel of God" a believing Jewish remnant within the broader Church of both Jews and Gentiles, a nonjudaizing group of Jewish Christians in Galatia, or an eschatological Israel that is to be saved at the time of Christ's return. Certain elements within Paul's other letters may be used to support one or the other of these views, but Galatians itself cannot easily be used in such a manner.

Rather, it seems better to argue that here Paul is using a self-designation of his Jewish-Christian opponents in Galatia—one that they used to identify their type of fulfilled Judaism vis-à-vis the official Judaism of their national compatriots (so, tentatively, Betz, *Galatians*, 323). Furthermore, this was a self-designation that they must have included in their message to Paul's Gentile converts, assuring them that by observing the God-given Jewish laws they would become fully "the Israel of God." The phrase itself is not found in the extant writings of Second Temple Judaism or later rabbinic Judaism, and does not appear elsewhere in Paul's letters. So it may be postulated that it arose amongst the Judaizers and became part of their message to Paul's Galatian converts. If that be the case, then Paul here climaxes his whole response to the judaizing threat in something of an ad hominem manner, implying in quite telling fashion that what the Judaizers were claiming to offer his converts they already have "in Christ" by faith: that they are truly children of Abraham together with all Jews who believe, and so properly can be called "the Israel of God" together with all Jews who believe.[34]

13. What does verse seventeen mean?

The marks of Yeshua for Paul were every scar that he got from escapes and stoning. These marks included being shunned by his friends and certainly by the Pharisees. He quit a nice life to become a poor evangelist to spread Yeshua's message.

Culture Section

Discussion

In the Near East, people carried articles on their back. Generally, the men carried the burden of wheat, grass, and stone used for building. Women carried home supplies, food, fuel and even water. Even children would carry what they could. In a caravan, if a person got ill, others who helped them to reach their destination would carry their burdens. A caravan would have to await sick members to recover. If not, then someone else had to carry their burden.

The powerful people imposed their burdens and work on the poor people when they were oppressed. A caravan of nobility or powerful people would have poor persons with them to carry their burden (their things) besides their own.

---

[34] Longenecker, R. N. (1990). *Galatians* (Vol. 41, pp. 298–299). Word, Incorporated.

Thoughts

Paul reminds this congregation, and other congregations in his letters, of all that he gave up becoming a follower and evangelist for Yeshua. He should be respected for the 100% turn around from persecutor to evangelist. Would you today have the courage to give up everything to become an evangelist for Christ? Not just for two years as the Mormons do, but for the rest of your life. Would you be willing to travel wherever Yeshua told you to go? These are difficult questions and easy to answer "yes" knowing that you will not be called. People in church today have that view. They can say "yes" with protecting feeling that they will never be called. However, sometimes you get what you request and remember who is calling.

Bibliography

A., Clines David J. *Word Biblical Commentary*. Nashville: T. Nelson, 2011.

Danker, Frederick W., and Bernard A. Taylor. *Biblical Greek Language and Lexicography: Essays in Honor of Frederick W. Danker*. Grand Rapids, MI: Wm. B. Eerdmans, 2004.

Errico, Rocco A., and George M. Lamsa. *Aramaic Light on Galatians through Hebrews: A Commentary Based on Aramaic, the Language of Jesus, and Ancient near Eastern Customs*. Smyma, GA: Noohra Foundation, 2005.

GotQuestions.org. "Home." GotQuestions.org, December 18, 2019. https://www.gotquestions.org/crucify-the-flesh.html.

GotQuestions.org. "Home." GotQuestions.org, February 5, 2010. https://www.gotquestions.org/life-Barnabas.html.

"Home." Bible Study. Accessed April 2, 2023. https://www.biblestudy.org/bibleref/meaning-of-numbers-in-bible/14.html.

"Home." Bible Study. Accessed March 27, 2023. https://www.biblestudy.org/bibleref/meaning-of-numbers-in-bible/15.html.

"Https://I.ytimg.com/Vi/W-TE_Ys4iwM/Maxresdefault.jpg." YouTube. YouTube, August 1, 2014. https://www.youtube.com/watch?v=ELQ20u19yXw.

"Marcionism." Wikipedia. Wikimedia Foundation, April 7, 2023. https://en.wikipedia.org/wiki/Marcionism.

Paul's first visit to Galatia, A.D. 51 or 52. Accessed March 27, 2023. https://biblehub.com/sermons/auth/lightfoot/paul's_first_visit_to_galatia_ad_51_or_52.htm.

Revandybooks. "St Paul and the Spirit. It Was Central to Paul's Faith." Bible in brief, November 6, 2018. https://www.bibleinbrief.org/2018/11/06/paul-and-the-spirit/.

"Who Was Titus in the Bible - Book of Titus in the Bible." biblestudytools.com, December 21, 2022. https://www.biblestudytools.com/bible-study/topical-studies/who-was-titus-in-the-bible-and-why-should-you-read-his-book-now.html.

"'Walk in the Spirit' - Galatians 5:16 Meaning and Application Today." biblestudytools.com, September 23, 2020. https://www.biblestudytools.com/bible-study/topical-studies/what-does-it-mean-to-walk-in-the-spirit.html.